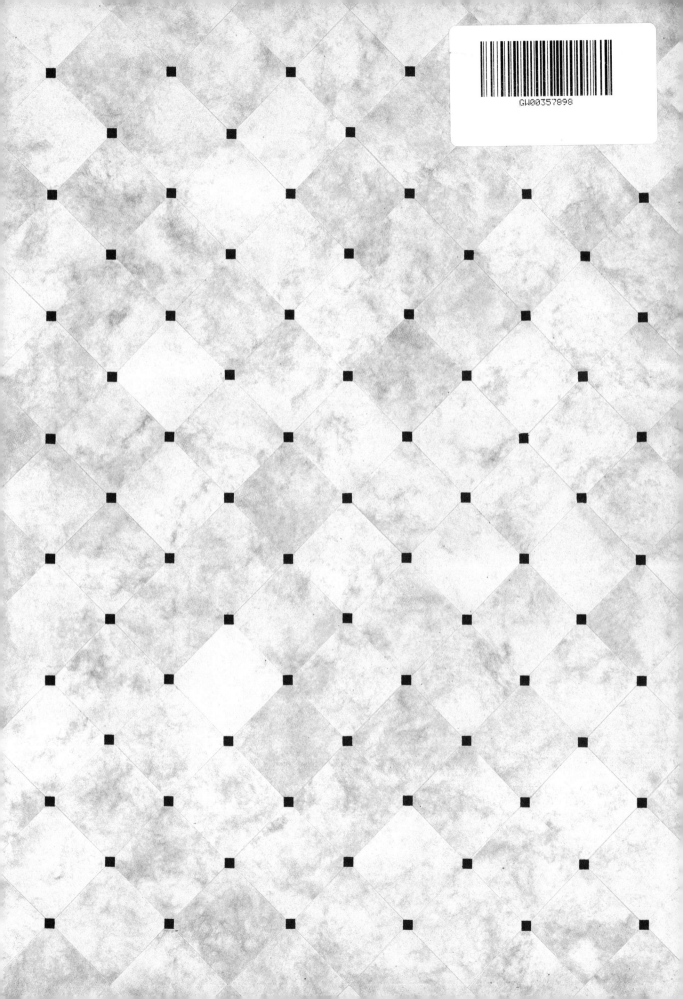

ITALIAN REGIONAL COOKING

ITALIAN REGIONAL COOKING

SIMONETTA LUPI VADA

WITH INTRODUCTORY TEXT BY LINDA SONNTAG

WARD LOCK

A QUARTO BOOK

Copyright © Quarto Publishing Limited

First published in Great Britain in 1987 by Ward Lock Limited,
8 Clifford Street, London WIX IRB, an Egmont Company.

British Library Cataloguing in Publication Data
Simonetta Lupi Vada
Italian Regional Cookery
 I. Cookery, Italian
 I. Title
 641.5945   TX723

ISBN 0 7063 6539 9

This book was designed and produced by
Quarto Publishing Limited
The Old Brewery
6 Blundell Street, London N7 9BH

Senior Editor Tessa Rose
Art Editor Nick Clark
Editors Susie Ward, Lorraine Dickey

Translator Anna Nyburg
Design Assistant Penny Dawes, Ursula Dawson
Illustration Mick Hill

Art Director Alastair Campbell
Editorial Director Carolyn King

Typeset by Dimension Ltd, London
Manufactured in Hong Kong by Regent Publishing Services Limited
Printed by Lee Fung Asco Printers Ltd, Hong Kong

CONTENTS

The cooking of Italy is the mother of all European cuisine, a fact acknowledged by even the 'Larousse Gastronomique'. Its origins are well recorded by the writers of ancient Rome, who have left very vivid impressions of the orgies indulged in by the ruling classes — but this is only half the picture.

THE ORIGINS OF ITALIAN COOKING

For while the aristocracy sat down, or rather reclined, to such dishes as peacock dressed in all its feathers or boar stuffed with live thrushes, the common soldier was roasting his ration of millet on a stone set in the campfire. When it was done, he crushed it, boiled it up with water and ate it as gruel. What was left over solidified into a cake and was consumed cold. This primitive meal was called *pulmentum*, and it has survived right up to the present day in the tastier form of polenta, whereas the more excessive dishes of the Empire, though more memorable, declined and fell with it.

Though what endured was, like polenta, deeply rooted in peasant life, the extravagance of Imperial tables is impossible to ignore. Flamingos and herons were also served up in their plumage; hedgehogs, puppies, wolves and donkeys enjoyed great popularity; dormice were kept in a barrel to stop them losing weight by exercise and were fed until they were fat, then roasted in honey and herbs. A favourite banquet recipe was 'Trojan pork'. The title referred to the horse of Troy, which had concealed the ambushing Greek soldiers. Trojan pork was stuffed with oysters and songbirds. One side of it was smeared with meal soaked in wine and oil and roasted, then the pig was turned over and the uncooked side was dipped into boiling water until it was done. Among the more exotic delicacies of the day were camel's foot and elephant's trunk.

All these things were consumed in stupendous quantities by the few who could afford them. The Emperor Maximinius is reputed to have eaten over 40 lb of meat a day, and to have drunk 35 pints of wine.'The Emperor Aurelian commissioned an actor, Farone, to amuse him by eating in one session a whole sheep, a whole sucking pig and a whole boar, accompanied by 100 buns and 100 bottles of wine.

The ancient Romans were fond of cooking with all the herbs and spices to which their vast empire gave them access. The original Roman seasoning was salt, evapo-

The artist Longlin's depiction of a sumptuous 18th century banquet, held in Venice in honour of the visiting Elector of Cologne.

rated from the water at the mouth of the river Tiber. It was used as a preservative for meat, and when more was made than could be used at home it became the basis for Rome's first important export trade, carried out of the city along the via Salaria — the Salt Road — which remains to this day.

To make salted meat more palatable, the Romans later added honey, dried fruit and spices. The resulting taste was the ancestor of today's agrodolce, a bittersweet sauce enjoyed with many different foods, including game and cabbage. A less attractive flavouring that seems to have been used liberally to disguise the taste of salt meat was *garum,* which one writer described as a sauce made from the entrails of mackerel.

Poultry could be reared by every household and there was a plentiful supply of chickens from Roman markets. Guinea fowl, pigeon and duck were also popular, and when the Romans conquered Gaul they discovered a great liking for goose. Consequently the returning troops drove huge flocks of geese from Picardy to Rome, living off the fields and causing much devastation as they went.

During the 2nd century the Emperor Trajan built the Forum, and next to it on Quirinal Hill a supermarket, a semi-circular structure with both open-air and closed booths. Behind it rambled multi-storey buildings housing more shops and stalls. There the Romans bought and sold meat and poultry, fish and wine. Olive oil was imported from Spain, wheat from Egypt and spices from Asia.

Cabbage was grown by the better-off, while the poor ate beans, mallow and a species of nettle. Spinach was not known till the 9th century, when it was introduced from Persia. Persia also provided Italy with melons, which farmers began to cultivate at Cantalupo, outside Rome. Figs and wild cherries were highly-prized natives.

Honey was used as a sweetener — even

on savoury foods. The Roman dish of honeyed eggs, *ova mellita,* gave its name to today's omelette. Another food given the sweet treatment was cheese. Flour and crushed fresh cheese were mixed with honey and eggs and baked in an earthenware mould — the cheesecake was born. The crushed fresh cheese in question was the ancestor of ricotta, but the Romans had a dozen varieties of cheese, of which they were very fond.

In the 3rd century AD Rome fell to the barbarians and the excesses of the degenerate empire were replaced by a more sober lifestyle. Recipes were preserved, as were other writings, in monasteries. In the 9th century came the Islamic invasion, which brought a new injection of life into Italian cooking. The Arabs brought with them the techniques of making ice cream and sorbet, and introduced desserts and sweet cakes made with marzipan. They were also responsible for planting the first sugar cane in Europe, but its cultivation did not really catch on until 200 years later, when cane and refined sugar were brought back by the Crusaders. Sugar went under the name of 'Indian salt' and was used as salt was, to season fish and meat. The Crusaders also reintroduced the spices that had been known in the days of ancient Rome, and a new interest in cooking sprang up. Milk and egg pies, vegetable tarts and bread sweetened with dried fruit appeared in a recipe book around 1290, along with the first-ever mention of pasta.

When Marco Polo opened up the spice trade between Venice and the Far East, Venetians grew fat on the profits and Venice became a centre of gastronomy. It was there that the table fork became popular and that drinking vessels were first made of fine glass.

In 16th century Florence the first modern cooking academy was set up. Called *Compagnia del Paiolo* (Company of the

Cauldron), one of its members was the painter Andrea del Sarto, who presented his colleagues with an exhibition dish made of gelatine in the shape of a temple held up by pillars of sausages and parmesan. Inside was a book with pages of pasta, and in front stood roasted thrushes, singing notes inscribed on the pasta in peppercorns.

In 1533 Catherine de Medici journeyed from Florence to France to marry the future King Henri II. France was still in the dark ages as far as the art of cooking was concerned, and Catherine took with her her own chefs and pastrycooks, who were adept at making ices, cakes and cream puffs. Marie de Medici followed in her footsteps in 1600 to become the bride of Henri IV. The Florentines were responsible for introducing haricot beans, petit pois, broccoli, artichokes and savoy cabbage to the French, and they also educated them in the culinary skills that were soon to make their own cuisine great and renowned the world over.

From Italy too came the double boiler. The French adopted it as the bain marie, but the original Mary's bath or *bagno maria* was named after its inventor Maria de Cleofsa, an alchemist who devised it to help her with her arcane researches into the relationship between magic, medicine and cooking.

The 16th century saw the arrival of the first tomato in Italy, brought back to Europe with the first red pepper from Mexico by the Spanish conquistadors. Called the *pomo d'oro* (golden apple), it was a cherry-sized yellow fruit used as a salad vegetable. It took 200 years for the large luscious red varieties to be developed for use in cooking.

Coffee was imported from the East. In 1585 Venice's ambassador to Turkey described to the Senate 'the habit of the Turks of drinking a black water as hot as you can bear it, taken from seeds called *cavee*, and they say it has the power of keeping men awake'. Its popularity was quickly esta-

blished in Venice and soon spread all over Europe.

The arrival of the potato was greeted with less enthusiasm. Pope Clement VII's botanist classified the specimen presented to him as 'a small truffle' and thenceforward it was cultivated in Italian gardens — as a decorative plant. The Italians were not alone in their confusion as to what to do with the potato — Queen Elizabeth I's chef threw away the tubers and served up the leaves. Potatoes never became a staple in Italy, even when their true use was discovered. Corn, the last major import, which came from America, provided a more popular alternative form of starch.

By the 16th century the French had become so advanced in the art of cooking that chefs from the French court were sent back to Venice to demonstrate their skills. The Venetians were not impressed. 'French cooks have ruined the Venetian stomach, 'wrote Gerolamo Zanetti, 'with so much porcherie (filth)... sauces, broths, extracts... garlic and onion in every dish... meat and fish transformed to such a point that they are scarcely recognizable by the time they get to the table... Everything mashed and mixed up with a hundred herbs, spices, sauces...'

Though the author was a biased (Venetian) observer writing some 400 years ago, his comment serves to underline the major difference between present-day Italian and French cooking. For while French cuisine tends to be elaborate and subtle, that of Italy is bold, simple and direct. Zanetti's mistrust of foreigners' meddling with good basic ingredients, transforming them into something 'scarcely recognizable', also shows a fierce respect for local tradition that is very much part of Italian cooking today. It is not just influence from abroad that is resisted, but influence from other regions of Italy, and it is this that makes Italian cooking so varied and so unique.

Italian cooking is the cooking of its regions. Until 1861 the regions of Italy were separate and often hostile states. Geographically as well as politically isolated from each other, each region developed its own entirely distinctive culinary character and traditions, traditions that are fiercely and proudly preserved today.

THE FLAVOURS OF ITALY

In Italy what is local is best. An Emilian would regard a salami produced in neighbouring Tuscany with scepticism; a Tuscan might smile ruefully at the Emilian's extravagant use of butter and cream. It follows that the traveller intent on enjoying Italian food should always order what the locals eat. It is no good asking for osso buco in Naples or beefsteak in Genoa, because they will be but pale imitations of the genuine things to be had in Milan and Florence — and you will have missed the opportunity to sample the perfect spaghetti alla marinara and torta pasqualina.

Italian pride in local fare and disdain of 'imports,' be they from only a few miles away, is soundly rooted in a love of fresh food. If there is one aspect of cooking shared by all the regions of Italy, it is the importance placed on the quality of the ingredients. Fruit and vegetables must be home-grown, preferably without chemical fertilizers, and picked at the peak of ripeness and glossy perfection. A squeeze of lemon juice is known to have more zest when the lemon is freshly picked from the tree and still warm from the sun, than when it has travelled long distances, ripening slowly in a crate. Meat should be home-reared and home-killed, and fish straight from the catch — seafood is rarely served at any distance from the coast.

All over Italy, Italians treat their food with respect. Their cooking is designed to emphasize the natural flavours of the ingredients. In this it is very different from French cooking, with its subtle harmonies and sophisticated sauces. Italian food is brightly coloured in the market place, and just as brightly coloured when it reappears on the plate. It is good, wholesome, hearty and endlessly varied — essentially home cooking that requires very few special skills to master.

The main meal in Italy is eaten in the middle of the day and can consist of several courses. First there may be a soup. This is usually a clear broth made substantial with rice or pasta, shredded vegetables or the dumplings made of potato or semolina called gnocchi. An alternative to soup would

*T*he food shops of Bologna, which is
renowned as the gastronomic capital of
Italy, are Aladdin's caves for the gourmet.
A dazzling display of sausages, cheeses,
mushrooms, preserved fruits and pickled
vegetables compete for the shopper's
attention.

be a risotto or a dish of baked or boiled pasta with a piquant or creamy sauce. Generous helpings of freshly grated parmesan cheese top this first course. Next comes a dish of fish or meat. In some areas the meat would be quite plainly cooked, perhaps grilled with aromatic olive oil and herbs as its only added flavouring; in others it might be a more complicated dish layered with melting cheese and tender ham, coated in breadcrumbs and fried in pork fat until succulent and golden.

A contorno - literally a contour — of seasonal vegetables or salad can be served with or after this course. To finish with, there will be fruit and local cheese, and the meal is of course accompanied by the wine of the region.

On Sundays or special occasions lunch may begin with antipasti — a selection of salami, fish, olives, artichokes and other savoury appetizers both hot and cold — and end with one of Italy's famous desserts, ices, cakes or pastries and black espresso coffee and liqueurs.

Lazio, Umbria and the Marches

This central band across the knee of Italy is dominated by the capital, Rome. The Roman appetite is robust and hearty, and the food that satisfies it is both good and simple. Sucking pig stuffed with herbs and roasted on a spit is a typical favourite dish. The Roman gastronomic calendar moves from festival to festival, with roast capon at Christmas, stuffed with breadcrumbs, salami, giblets and cheese; sucking lamb at Easter, and on Midsummer Night, snails in a sauce of garlic, anchovy, tomato and mint.

In Rome you can eat both the fresh home-made pasta of the north, in a justly famous dish of cannelloni — flat pasta sheets rolled round a meat filling — and the dried tubular

THE REGIONS OF ITALY

The regions listed below represent the main geographical divisions of Italy. The shields shown are those of the main town or city in each region. Each recipe is accompanied by one of these shields to denote its known, or suspected, origin.

KEY TO REGIONS

LAZIO, UMBRIA AND THE MARCHES
(See below left)

TUSCANY
(See p.16)

EMILIA-ROMAGNA
(See p.18)

LIGURIA
(See p.20)

VENETO
(See p.21)

LOMBARDY
(See p.23)

PIEDMONT
(See p.26)

SICILY
(See p.29)

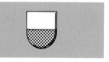

NAPLES AND THE SOUTH: CAMPANIA, CALABRIA, BASILICATA, APULIA AND ABRUZZI-MOLISE
(See p.26)

SARDINIA
(See p.29)

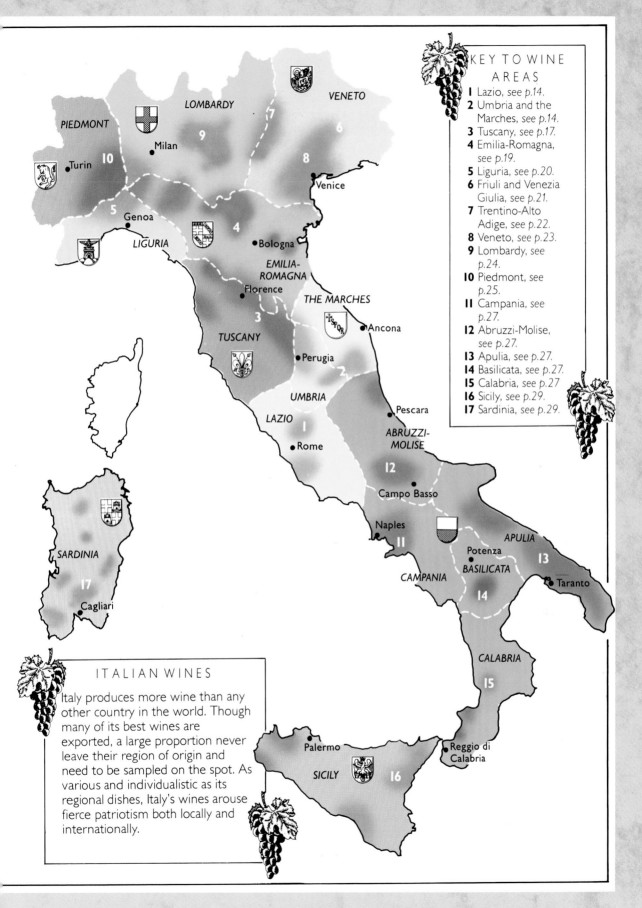

PIEDMONT

Turin

LOMBARDY

Milan

VENETO

Venice

LIGURIA

Genoa

EMILIA-
ROMAGNA

Bologna

Florence

THE MARCHES

Ancona

TUSCANY

Perugia

UMBRIA

LAZIO

Rome

ABRUZZI-
MOLISE

Pescara

Campo Basso

Naples

CAMPANIA

SARDINIA

Cagliari

APULIA

Potenza

BASILICATA

Taranto

CALABRIA

Reggio di
Calabria

Palermo

SICILY

KEY TO WINE AREAS

1 Lazio, see p.14.
2 Umbria and the Marches, see p.14.
3 Tuscany, see p.17.
4 Emilia-Romagna, see p.19.
5 Liguria, see p.20.
6 Friuli and Venezia Giulia, see p.21.
7 Trentino-Alto Adige, see p.22.
8 Veneto, see p.23.
9 Lombardy, see p.24.
10 Piedmont, see p.25.
11 Campania, see p.27.
12 Abruzzi-Molise, see p.27.
13 Apulia, see p.27.
14 Basilicata, see p.27.
15 Calabria, see p.27
16 Sicily, see p.29.
17 Sardinia, see p.29.

ITALIAN WINES

Italy produces more wine than any other country in the world. Though many of its best wines are exported, a large proportion never leave their region of origin and need to be sampled on the spot. As various and individualistic as its regional dishes, Italy's wines arouse fierce patriotism both locally and internationally.

THE WINES OF LAZIO, UMBRIA AND THE MARCHES

LAZIO

Lazio has two main wine-producing areas: the Castelli Romani in the hills around Rome and the area around Lake Bolsena, about 60 miles from it.

CASTELLI ROMANI

This is an area of 50 square miles in the Alban hills producing mainly white wine that can be either sweet or dry. The grapes for the sweet wine are allowed to dry out a little on the vine before they are picked and fermented in the caves of the Alban hills. The sweet wines go well with fresh fruit and the dry complement robust Roman pasta dishes and their suckling pigs and baby lambs. The best known of these wines is Frascati, clear gold in color and either dry, semi-sweet or sweet.

CASTELBRACCIANO

A sweet, golden-yellow wine from the shores of Lake Bracciano.

CASTRENSE

Light red and white wines from the shores of Lake Bolsena.

CECUBO

A wine from Gaeta drunk by Cicero and Horace. It is a very light red with a full fragrance.

EST! EST!! EST!!!

There is a curious tale of how this wine came by its name. Local legend has it that an 18th century cardinal on a journey round Italy sent his steward before him to try out the wines in various hostelries. When the steward discovered a good one, he was to chalk 'Est!' ('It is') on the door. At Montefiascone he was so impressed that he chalked 'Est! Est!! Est!!!' before passing out into a stupor. The cardinal arrived and his enthusiasm for the wine was so great that he drank himself to death on it there and then.

UMBRIA AND THE MARCHES

Wine production here is not extensive. The hillsides are very steep and in many cases vines are grown alternating with rows of corn. Both red and white are generally on the rough side, but there are two notable exceptions — Verdicchio dei Castelli di Jesi from the Marches, and Orvieto from Umbria.

ALTE VALLE DEL TENERE

The wines of the upper Tiber, both red and white, are light and simple and ideal for lunch.

BIANCHELLO

A light dry white from the Marches, it goes well with fish.

ORVIETO

Made mainly from the Trebbiano grape, this wine has been produced around the cathedral city of Orvieto for at least 500 years. There are two straw-coloured whites, one dry and the other semi-sweet. The grapes for the semi-sweet are allowed to begin to rot after they have been picked — in the German Auslese the grapes start to rot on the vine — and the resulting wine is not too sweet to be drunk with fish or poultry. The dry Orvieto is the more popular export.

VERDICCHIO DEI CASTELLI DI JESI

This wine is drunk along the holiday coast around Rimini and is also exported in large quantities. It is one of the very best of the Italian whites, despite the vulgar bottle. Straw-coloured and slightly bitter, the best Verdicchio has a secondary fermentation like Chianti.

VIN COTTO

'Cooked wine' is made by reducing must over heat and then topping it up with uncooked must. The wine is fermented and kept for two years. It is strong, rich and sweet.

The Italians' passion for ice cream dates back to the days of the Roman empire, when snow and crushed berries were served at the imperial table.

pasta of the south. Sauces include tuna and mushrooms (alla carrettiera), hot red peppers (all'arrabbiata - rabid!) and the celebrated alla carbonara, made with salt pork, eggs and cream.

Saltimbocca, the picturesque name meaning 'jump in the mouth', is slices of ham atop slices of veal, flavoured with sage, fried in butter and then braised in white wine. Stracciatella is another well-known dish, a clear soup with a mixture of eggs, flour and cheese poured into it. It breaks up as it cooks, forming the 'little rags' that give the soup its name.

For dessert you might be offered zuppa inglese, neither soup nor English, but a rich trifle flavoured with rum.

The mountainous region of Umbria is the biggest producer — and hence consumer — of meat in the whole of Italy. There is plenty of game in the higher regions, sheep and goats a little further down and cattle and pigs on the foothills. The pork in particular is

excellent. The animals are fattened on acorns and much of the meat is cured and turned into sausages spiced with garlic, pepper, pine nuts and fennel.

Umbria is famed even in France for its superb truffles, eaten sliced on pasta, and for its freshwater fish, in particular the roach. The capital of Umbria is Perugia, which is reckoned to manufacture the best chocolates in the world.

Most of the inhabitants of the Marches live along the coast, and it follows that fish is the staple of their diet. Each seaside town has its own way of making fish soup, with the ingredients varying according to the day's catch. Snails flavoured with fennel, and huge fat olives — stuffed, rolled in breadcrumbs and fried — are other delicacies to be had in the region, while Urbino in the north is distinguished by its sauce. It was first invented by a Duke of Urbino in the 15th century, who was so afraid of being poisoned that he refused to let his chef season his food. Once the food had been tasted for him he added his own sauce, prepared according to a secret recipe by a servant whom he trusted.

The recipe was recently rediscovered and the sauce is produced today in a bottle with the Duke's portrait on the label. His profile is disfigured by the removal of the bridge of his nose — a piece of self-inflicted surgery. The Duke's right eye was blinded by the claws of a falcon, and he had the top of his nose cut away so that he could see with his left eye if a would-be assassin was attempting to sneak up on him from the right.

Tuscany

Tuscany is the heart of Italy. Its food is simply prepared and with the best ingredients. Elaborate dishes have no place on the menu here; indeed the Tuscan way of cooking is sometimes looked upon by outsiders as austere because of its conspicuous lack of complicated sauces and seasonings.

Florence is the capital and, in culinary terms, Florentine (alla fiorentina) is synonymous with spinach. But this is only outside Italy — to an Italian 'alla fiorentina' simply means 'in the Florentine style'. Bistecca alla fiorentina is a typical Tuscan dish well worth travelling miles to sample in its native city — it is simply prepared with ingredients of the highest quality, and it does not contain spinach. Bistecca alla fiorentina is steak from a choice two-year old Chiana Valley bull, grilled briefly above chestnut wood. It is salted and rubbed with a little olive oil just before it is removed from the fire and served perhaps with fresh beans.

Tuscans are known throughout Italy as mangiafagioli (bean eaters). They eat beans in soup, beans in risotto and beans with pasta. Beans and tuna fish is a favourite appetizer. Fagioli nel fiasco is beans cooked slowly in a closed flask to prevent the flavour from escaping. They are then eaten simply with

Pesaro, like all Italian coastal towns, has its own recipe for fish soup, the ingredients for which vary from day to day according to the fishermen's catch.

THE WINES OF TUSCANY

The landscape of Tuscany used to reflect the diet of its inhabitants: bread, olive oil and wine. Corn, olive trees and vines would be grown in the same field, with perhaps a cow or two wandering among them. The peasants had to give half their produce to the landowners and could not risk a single crop. Now the vines have taken over in rows well-spaced enough to allow the passage of a tractor. Still, a few farmers have kept their olive trees, as much because the grey-green colour is a vital part of the landscape as for their oil.

ARBIA

A dry white wine that goes well with the pecorino — sheeps cheese — of the region. A 'virgin' wine, because the must is fermented without stalks or skin.

BRUNELLO DI MONTALCINO

One of the great Italian reds — full and fragrant, smooth and well balanced, it is aged in the cask for five or six years and enthusiasts recommend keeping it in the bottle for up to 50.

CANDIA

Sweet red and white wines from the northwest of the region.

CHIANTI

Baron Bettino Ricasoli 'invented' Chianti in the 1860s. When his young wife danced at a ball with a man who seemed to be paying her too much attention, he called her away and they drove all night to Brolio, where there was a gloomy castle the baron's family had not lived in for years. Here they set up a permanent home well away from the temptations of society. The baron diverted himself by developing a new wine — a mixture of black Sangiovese and white Malvasia grapes, and a method of making them ferment twice, giving the wine a novel taste and a slight tingle. When the first fermentation is over, a rich must from dried grapes is added to the wine, inducing a second fermentation that lasts from two to three weeks. Wines made by this method are drunk young and sold in typical Chianti flasks covered in wicker (or plastic). Finer Chiantis meant to be aged are only fermented once and sold in ordinary claret bottles. Chianti is produced and exported on a very large scale, but Chianti classico comes only from the area between Florence and Siena and bears the growers' label of a black cockerel against a gold background.

MOSCADELLO DI MONTALCINO

A light, golden, fragrant wine with a slight tingle, drunk young and chilled.

UGOLINO BIANCO

A clear straw-coloured white from near Livorno. To be drunk young and chilled with fish.

VAL DI CHIANA

A clear, golden-yellow wine, a 'virgin' like Arbia, see above.

VERNACCIA DI SAN GIMIGNANO

A fresh, straw-coloured wine with a hint of bitterness comes from around this picturesque town, which has been completely overtaken by tourism. It is a fine, dry white that improves with age.

VIN NOBILE DI MONTEPULCIANO

A smooth, well-balanced ruby red wine with a hint of violet, best after at least five years in the bottle.

VIN SANTO

A rich, sweet dessert wine, very popular in Tuscany.

The Ponte Vecchio in Florence, the city whose chefs and pastry cooks were responsible for educating the French in the culinary arts.

olive oil, salt, pepper and lemon juice and a loaf of flat Tuscan bread.

The bread in Tuscany is unsalted, as it forms a component part of so many dishes that a too-salty flavour would ruin. There is, for example, a bread salad, tossed with tomatoes, cucumber and pink onions, and a bread and tomato soup, especially beloved by children. The other reason that bread is not salted is that salt absorbs moisture, and bread is bought in big enough quantities to last a week. Salted bread would go mouldy before the week was out. The Tuscans are a practical and economy-conscious people.

They are very fond of game, particularly pheasant and hare, which is plentiful in the hillsides, and which they serve simply roasted and flavoured with wild rosemary. Their pecorino cheese with its sharp flavour and black crust is one of the best in Italy and is an excellent accompaniment to Chianti,

Tuscany's famous wine.

There are two more specialties of the region that deserve a mention — Livorno's splendid fish soup, cacciucco alla livornese, and Siena's flat dessert cake, panforte, full of dried fruit, almonds and spices, often taken home by tourists as a souvenir of the lovely medieval city that makes it.

Emilia-Romagna

This rich and fertile region lying to the north of Tuscany is Italy's land of plenty, and not for nothing is its capital, Bologna, known as Bologna la grassa - 'the fat'. Bologna is the home of mortadella, perhaps Italy's finest sausage, and, above all, fresh pasta. Made from local wheat milled very fine, bolognese pasta is rolled out so thinly you can almost see through it, cut into long narrow strips to make tagliatelle and served with a tasty ragù, which comes from the French word ragoût, or stew. It is said that the inventor of tagliatelle was inspired by the fine flaxen hair of Lucretia Borgia and that the inventor of tortellini, little stuffed rings of pasta, fell in love with his employer's wife when he saw her sleeping in the nude and promptly produced a new pasta in the shape of her navel.

Tortellini stuffed with turkey, sausage, ham, pork, egg and cheese are traditionally served on Christmas Day as a first course with a rich sauce of butter and cream and topped with grated cheese. Lasagne, baked in the oven with layers of meat and cream sauces, and cappelletti, 'little hats,' stuffed with ricotta, chicken, egg and spices, are other popular forms of pasta in Bologna.

Emilians are very fond of veal and serve it in their typically extravagant way, stuffed with cheeese and ham and braised in wine, a habit that would horrify their plainer-living Tuscan neighbours.

In Emilia is the city of Parma, renowned throughout the world for is proscuitto or Parma ham, and for having given its name to parmesan cheese. The original Parmesan is made in Reggio nell'Emilia and is known variously as parmigiano reggiano or formaggio di grana, 'grained cheese,' because of its finely-grained texture.

From Modena comes zampone, stuffed foreleg of pork, and from Piacenza bomba

THE WINES OF EMILIA-ROMAGNA

The wines of this region are not as full and flavoursome as its cooking. Its most famous wine is Lambrusco, a dry sparkling red, beloved by the Bolognese and arousing strong reactions in visitors from outside the region, who are either captivated or repelled.

ALBANA

A well-balanced, yellow-gold wine grown around the town of Bertinoro. Light and fresh with a slight sweetness, but nevertheless delicious with fish.

CASTELFRANCO

A fragrant dry white wine from around Modena, made from a mixture of grapes grown in the same vineyard.

GUTTURNIO

A dryish, ruby-red wine, best drunk very young and served cool, made mainly from Barbera grapes.

LAMBRUSCO

Dry, red and sparkling, very pink and frothy when poured, but the bubbles subside to a tingle. The Bolognese say that its fresh, clean taste complements their rich cooking and that it aids the digestion.

SANGIOVESE

A fresh, ruby-red wine with a hint of garnet, widely-grown throughout the region. Fruity when young, it mellows with age and is well prized by the locals.

SCANDIANO BIANCO

A popular, straw-yellow wine, this is not renowned for its quality outside the region. There are still dry and sparkling sweet varieties.

TREBBIANO

This grape is widely grown in the region, producing wines of different style and quality. The more common variety is drunk young, but there is also a sharp elegant wine that goes well with fish and a sweeter, sparkling Trebbiano for dessert.

THE WINES OF LIGURIA

Liguria is a small region and an even smaller wine producer, with most of the vineyards growing enough to supply only their owners' tables. Genoa is the center of the Italian wine trade, but it deals in the wines of the rest of Italy and drinks its own at home.

BARBAROSSA

So called because of the way the grape grows in 'red beards'. A festive pink wine, there is also a sweet variety.

CAMPOCHIESA BIANCO

A full-flavoured dry white wine from the Pigato grape, Campochiesa improves with age. Traditionally it is laid down at the birth of a son to be drunk at his wedding.

CINQUETERRE

Drunk young, this is a delicate, clear, yellow-gold wine with a slightly bitter taste, made from the Vernaccia grape. It comes from five villages — hence its name — high up in rocky terrain. There is a sweet variety made from grapes part-dried in the sun. It has a high alcohol content (16°) and is much enjoyed with ice cream.

CORONATA

A dry white wine with a sharp fresh taste that goes very well with fish.

DOLCEACQUA

Made mainly from Rosesse grapes, this is a full, heavy, aromatic wine that goes well with stronger-flavoured local dishes, such as pesto.

di riso, a pudding-shaped mould of rice cooked in white wine that contains vegetables and pigeons cooked in red wine. In Ferrara the local delicacy is grilled eel and at Ravenna you can sample another Italian fish soup, brodetto.

Liguria

This is the narrow strip of coast that stretches from San Remo to La Spezia and is bordered to the north by the Alps and Apeninnes. Its capital is the great port of Genoa and its culinary traditions, not surprisingly, reflect the seafaring nature of its inhabitants. For the fishermen who spent weeks at sea, food had to be prepared to keep. Lentils, chickpeas and dried beans, pies and biscuits were eaten at sea and when they returned home, the sailors satisfied their cravings for fresh green vegetables with tarts filled with artichokes, spinach, courgettes, Swiss chard and wild herbs — torta pasqualina. Genoa's favourite herb is basil, the main ingredient for pesto sauce. The word comes from 'pestle'. Basil, garlic, parmesan, olive oil and pine nuts — and sometimes lemon rind, beans and potatoes — are pounded together with a pestle in a mortar and served with gnocchi or pasta.

The land of Liguria is not good farming land, so every little bit of vegetation must be put to good use. One recipe calls for wild herbs, 'the kind you find growing on the garden wall'. The Ligurian frugality was responsible for the invention of ravioli — the word comes from robiole, or leftovers — little scraps stuffed into envelopes of pasta. Cappon magro is a true Genoese joke. Literally 'thin capon', it is a dish that contains no meat at all. It is, for all that, a very majestic concoction and has been pronounced worthy of Homeric heroes. Layered boiled vegetables and pickled fish are built up to form a huge colourful dome

Venice is a city of exotic culinary contrasts, a legacy from its position at the centre of the spice trade in the Middle Ages. Here, some of the finest restaurants in Europe pay as much attention to the preparation of risi e bisi, a simple dish of rice and peas, as they do to scampi, oysters and caviar. Risi e bisi was, after all, the favourite dish of the Doges.

which is then draped in a green sauce flavoured with herbs.

Veneto

Veneto, with Trentino to the west and Friuli-Venezia Giulia to the East, is one of Italy's major wine producing areas and its famous exports include Soave, Valpolicella and Bardolino. Its gastronomic centre is its capital, Venice, whose cuisine still reflects the legacy of the medieval spice trade. Here you can enjoy lightly-curried fish and a delicate dish of peppered calves liver and onions. The Venetians' taste is, on the whole, exotic. They like rice with scampi, cuttlefish, or prawns in a garlic and tomato sauce, and even rice with grapes, cheese and garlic. Salt cod is cooked with cinnamon, turkey with pomegranate sauce and courgette flowers are fried in butter.

Pasta is not much eaten in Veneto. Instead the locals favour polenta, which is not yellow

THE WINES OF FRIULI-VENEZIA GIULIA

The character of this region is more Slavic than Italian and the inhabitants are less patriotic than anywhere else in Italy. You are quite as likely to be served a Yugoslavian wine or a wine from Veneto as one grown locally.

GAMAY

A brilliant ruby-red wine from vines imported from France. Gamay grows well on the hills of the region and has a faint strawberry taste when young.

PICCOLIT

A golden-yellow dessert wine drunk chilled. It was much admired in European courts at the turn of the century and is best when it has aged a few years in the bottle. Piccolit grapes are part-dried in the sun after being picked to give the wine a more concentrated sweetness.

PINOT GRIGIO

Arguably the best white wine of the region, it has a slightly pink tinge and a faint tang of nutmeg. There are also smooth red and spumante versions.

SAUVIGNON

Another grape imported from France and grown widely throughout the region. An elegant, straw-yellow wine with a slightly bitter aftertaste.

TOCAI

A dry yellow-white wine quite unlike the Hungarian Tokay, which is a great dessert wine. Makes a very good accompaniment to fish dishes.

Lombardy is a region of dairy farms and rice production. It is famous for gorgonzola and bel paese cheese and for its tradition of long, slow cooking, which survives not only in small hilltop towns like this one but also in the region's capital, Milan.

THE WINES OF TRENTINO — ALTO ADIGE

Alto Adige, which its inhabitants call the South Tyrol, is German-speaking, and the wines have German names and are exported to Germany, Switzerland and Austria. The wines are finer and quite distinct from those produced in Trentino, which are less numerous.

BLAUBURGUNDER

A reliable, full red wine from the Pinot noir grape grown around Bolzano, Caldaro and Terlano.

CALDARO

Lago di Caldaro is a full red wine with a slight almond flavour. Often called Kalterersee, the German name for the lake.

COLLINE BOLZANO

Red wines grown on the hills around Bolzano from the Schiavone grape. Variable in quality.

GEWÜRZTRAMINER

In the South Tyrol is the village of Tramin, or Termeno, which the locals claim gave Gewürztraminer its name. But the white wine from this region is not as full or fragrant as its more famous namesake from Alsace.

RIESLING

A well-balanced wine, the Terlaner Riesling is one of the few whites of the area that are exported.

SANTA MAGDALENA

The finest red wine of this region — a brilliant ruby with a hint of orange, it is smooth with a slightly bitter aftertaste. Made from Schiava and Schiavone grapes and grown in the hills east of Bolzano.

THE WINES OF VENETO

One of the major wine-growing regions, Veneto produces Valpolicella, Bardolino and Soave, three of Italy's best known exports.

BARDOLINO

A bright, ruby-red wine with a fresh taste, made from a variety of grapes grown on the eastern shores of Lake Garda. Best drunk young and cool.

CABERNET

A full-bodied, vigorous red with a slight amber tint, best after it has spent at least three years in the bottle. It has woodland flavours of raspberry and honey with a hint of violet.

COLLI DI VALDOBBIADENE

A dry white with a hint of bitterness, and a sweet, slightly sparkling dessert wine, both bear this name.

MERLOT

A ruby-red wine with a fresh taste and a hint of almond. The Merlot grape is grown all over Italy; the Veneto Merlot is lighter than that from Trentino.

PROSECCO

A straw-yellow wine, aromatic and fresh. There is also a sparkling variety — Prosecco Spumante. Prosecco is grown all over the north of Italy.

RABOSO

A rather rough red wine common across the region, and best drunk young.

RECIOTO

A red wine, so-called because it is made only from the 'ears' (orecchie) of the bunches of grapes, which are riper than the rest. It is full and heavy and makes a good accompaniment to roast meat and mature cheese. A sweet sparkling variety can be drunk with dessert.

SOAVE

Smooth, dry and straw-yellow, this is one of the finest Italian whites. It is made mainly from Garganega grapes and is best drunk young and chilled as an accompaniment to the fish dishes of Venice.

VALPOLICELLA

Slightly fuller than Bardolino, this is the most popular red of the region. It can be aged in the bottle, but is perhaps best drunk cool and young.

as in most other parts of Italy, but white, made from the fine white maize grown in Friuli-Giulia. Another simple dish prized by the Venetians is risi e bisi, rice and peas. This falls somewhere between a soup and a risotto and is made at its best with the tender young peas available only in spring.

The merchants of Venice first introduced sugar into Europe and Venetians today still have a sweet tooth. In the middle of the morning the city is full of people sitting under awnings enjoying their 'ombrina' — 'little shade' — a glass of wine or a cup of coffee and sweet cornmeal biscuits or the vanilla cake called pandoro.

Lombardy

Lombardy's national dish is risotto alla milanese, rice delicately flavoured and coloured with saffron. Another speciality is osso buco, braised veal shank on the bone, of which the marrow is considered to be the tastiest part. To the Milanese goes the credit of inventing another famous meat dish, the Wiener Schnitzel. The original costoletta alla milanese, the breaded veal chop, was taken back to Vienna in the 19th century by General Radetzky, and the Viennese promptly adopted it as their own.

Milan is Italy's financial capital and though

the pace of life there is fast, cooking methods are traditionally slow and housewives spend long hours at the stove, braising, stewing, spit-roasting and gently simmering meat to succulent perfection. It is generally held in France that the Italians overcook their meat, and certainly they like it well done.

Though Lombardy is famous for its rice, it does not grow quite so much of it as Piedmont. It is primarily an area of wheat and dairy farming. Butter is the cooking medium and there are some excellent cheeses, among them gorgonzola. In Milan is the Via dei Ghiottoni, the street of gourmets (or gluttons), which is lined with food shops of every possible sort. One in particular, called Peck, is internationally renowned for its enormous selection of cheeses and its top-quality veal and cured meats. One of the more unusual of these is bresaola, beef salted and dried and sliced paper-thin to be eaten with olive oil, lemon juice and pepper.

Every visitor to Milan is sure to be offered a slice of panettone, a leavened cake made with eggs, raisins and candied peel that is the ideal breakfast accompaniment to a cup of coffee. Torrone is an almond-flavoured dessert cake that has been a popular treat since

THE WINES OF LOMBARDY

In the Valtelline, with the Alps to the north and the mountains of Bergamo to the south, the aristocratic Nebbiolo produces fine red wines as in Piedmont — Sassella, Grumello and Inferno. But they are quite elusive and inconsistent in quality and are often exported to Switzerland or appear under a brand name. The other main wine-producing areas are around Lake Garda and to the south of the Po in the Oltrepo Pavese.

CHIARETTO DEL GARDA

The red wines around Lake Garda are very light, and the rosés darker than the French ones. This is an intense pink wine made from a mixture of four types of grape. It has a sharp fresh taste and should be drunk young and cool. A good wine to choose for an outdoor lunch.

COLLINE DEL GARDA AND COLLINE MANTOVANE

Red, white and rosé wines from the area between Lake Garda and Mantua. The reds are very light and clear and all should be drunk young and cool.

FRANCIACORTA

A brilliant ruby-red wine with a fresh taste and a hint of raspberry.

FRECCIAROSSA

Frecciarossa is a village in the Oltrepo Pavese where the Odero family produce four fine wines bottled on their estate in the French style. Each has a brand name: the dry white is called 'La Vigne Blanche', the medium dry white 'Sillery', the rosé 'Saint George' and the red, considered one of the finest Italian reds, is named 'Le Grand Cru'.

LACRIMA VITIS

A golden dessert wine made from Moscato grapes, partly dried in the sun after picking.

LUGANA

A fresh, dry white made from Trebbiano grapes and aged in the cask before bottling. It has a pale golden colour and a slight saffron taste which goes very well with fish.

VALTELLINE REDS

Sassella, Grumello and Inferno are the great red wines of Lombardy, grown in terraces along the River Adda, which flows into Lake Como. They are made from 85 per cent of Nebbiolo grapes and benefit from ageing in the bottle. Drink them with grilled and roast meat and game.

THE WINES OF PIEDMONT

Fine wines have been grown in Piedmont since Roman times. The vineyards are gently sloping, the sun is not too fierce, and the vines are protected from the wind by the Alps. Most of the region's wine is full-bodied red, but it also produces the sparkling white Asti Spumante. Turin is the centre of vermouth production, which mostly uses the cheaper wine of Apulia. The vermouth's aroma comes from the herbs in the mountains nearby.

ASTI SPUMANTE

A sparkling, sweet white wine made from the Moscato grape, which is widely grown in Piedmont, Asti is made by the *cuve close* method — fermented in closed vats and bottled under pressure. This is quicker and cheaper than the *méthode champagnoise*, which involves secondary fermentation in the bottle, and which is also used in this region to produce some sparkling dry whites, for example Gancia Royal Cuvée. Asti is a classic dessert wine that can also be enjoyed mid-morning or at parties.

BARBARESCO

A full-bodied, deep red wine made from the Nebbiolo grape, it matures early, taking on a slight amber tint. It comes from the hilly country near Alba.

BARBERA

Piedmont's commonest wine, this is a red that varies greatly in quality. It can be slightly sparkling and sweet; it can be coarse when young or mellow with age. The best Barbera, from around Asti, is granted a growers' association label of blue grapes on the city's red tower.

BAROLO

One of Italy's great wines, Barolo is deep red when young and takes on an amber tinge with age. It is made from the Nebbiolo grape grown in the hills around Alba and is full and fragrant with a hint of violets. Barolo is particularly enjoyable with snails, game and mature cheese.

CORTESE DELL'ALTO MONFERRATO

A light, dry white to be drunk young with fish. A semi-sweet sparkling version is called Cortese di Gavi.

FREISA

A smooth, dry, garnet red wine from around Turin. It has a hint of raspberries and violets.

GATTINARA

A highly-prized garnet red wine with a hint of raspberries, Gattinara is preferred to Barolo by some connoisseurs. Made from the aristocratic Nebbiolo grape, it is best after three years in the bottle.

GRIGNOLINO D'ASTI

Rose-coloured and perfumed, from the Grignolino grape, this is a wine to be drunk young and cool with pasta or poultry.

MOSCATO D'ASTI

A cheaper, commoner version of Asti Spumante.

PASSITO DI CALUSO

A golden-yellow dessert wine, full, round and fruity, made from Erbulace grapes that have been partly dried in the sun after picking to concentrate their sweetness. Excellent with fresh white cheese.

THE FLAVOURS OF ITALY

the 13th century, and another favourite Lombardy dessert is pears stuffed with gorgonzola cheese.

Piedmont

Piedmont is a mainly mountainous region and, as in other places with similar terrains, its diet is substantial and sustaining. But its capital, Turin, also has a tradition of culinary sophistication inherited from its great ruling House of Savoy, and this gives Piedmontese cooking an edge of distinction lacking in other mountain areas. Side by side with robust dishes of lasagne, polenta, gnocchi and boiled mixed meats are delicacies such as trout baked on a bed of mushrooms, and bagna cauda, a hot sauce of olive oil, butter, garlic and pounded anchovies, eaten as a dip for cold vegetables, among which is the cardoon, or edible thistle.

Another speciality is fonduta, a kind of fondue made with fat fontina cheese, cornflour, milk and egg yolks, which is sometimes served poured over a slab of polenta and decorated with finely-sliced truffles.

The frogs that breed in the rice fields are served up, appropriately, in risotto, and every meal is accompanied by grissini, the long crisp bread sticks that have become synonymous with Italian eating throughout the world. For dessert you might be offered a rich confection of chestnuts and cream called monte bianco, and after the meal a glass of grappa.

Naples and the south

Naples is the gastronomic centre of the south, just as Bologna is of the north, and it sets the tone for the cooking of Calabria, Basilicata, Apulia and Abruzzi-Molise, as well as its own region of Campania. Campania is the south's most fertile region and grows wheat, maize and millet as well as huge crops of all kinds of vegetables, especially tomatoes. All the ingredients are to hand for Naples' most celebrated and most exported dish, pizza. In Naples seafood is plentiful and a favourite spaghetti sauce is con vongole, with clams. Campania breeds the large white buffaloes whose milk is turned into mozzarella.

Macugnaga in Piedmont, Italy's prime rice-producing region. The hills here abound in goats and wild boar, and in the woods grow white truffles, which are prized even in France.

THE WINES OF NAPLES AND THE SOUTH

CAMPANIA

Wine has been cultivated here since Roman times, but Campania is not a region renowned for its fine wines. Much of what it produces today is for blending, and a great deal of it, of course, supplies the local tourist trade.

AGLIANICO

A robust red from the grape of the same name, which is grown all over southern Italy.

CAPRI

Red, white and rosé wines come from the island, but there are also mainland wines bottled under the same name. The white is a straw-yellow with a fresh taste and a hint of bitterness and highly thought of by the locals. All three are acceptable table wines made from a mixture of grapes.

COLLI SORRENTINI AND SORRENTO

Red, white and rosé wines, some of which appear as 'Capri', or as 'Sorriso di Sorrento', which particularly appeals to the more romantic tourists.

FALERNO

Both dry and sweet, white and red wines come from the plain north of Naples. The white is straw-yellow with a hint of amber and full flavour.

ISCHIA

Ischia Bianco is a delicate white, drunk young and chilled. It is made from a mixture of Biancolella and Fontana grapes. The reds from the island are not quite so individual, some being rather coarse.

LACRIMA CHRISTI

This is a very popular wine because of its memorable name (tears of Christ), but only the dry, German-style white lives up to its reputation. Other wines, including reds and rosés grown on the slopes of Vesuvius, are sold under this name and can be disappointing.

ABRUZZI-MOLISE

Craggy and mountainous, this region is not a great wine producer. What it does produce is either drunk locally or sent north for blending.

ABRUZZI BIANCO

A sharp, fresh white from the Trebbiano grape that makes a good accompaniment to fish.

ABRUZZI ROSSO

From the Montepulciano grape, which is grown widely throughout the region, this is a very light red, sometimes with a slight tingle.

APULIA, BASILICATA, CALABRIA

In the hot south of Italy, wine production is the main source of income — in fact Apulia produces more wine than any other region of Italy. But because of the heavy soil and the fierce sun, and the fact that the vines are grown close to the ground so that extra heat is reflected up at them, the wine tends to be coarse and strong. The reds are used for blending and the whites as a base for the vermouth industry in Turin.

ALEATICO

A rich, sweet dessert wine from the grape of the same name. The must is taken off the skins of part-dried grapes and fermentation is halted by the addition of spirits. The result is quite strong (14°-17°).

CASTEL DEL MONTE

A fresh tingling white wine from the Bombino Bianco grape.

CASTELLANA

Red and rosé wines drunk very young and mainly used for blending.

LOCOROTONDO

Pips and skin are removed from a mixture of grapes to produce a characterless white wine used mainly as a base for vermouth.

Amalfi (above) was the first Italian maritime republic and dates back to the 6th century. It is famed for its fish restaurants and one of its specialities is a dish of spaghetti with octopus, anchovies, prawns and garlic. These extraordinary conical huts or 'trulli' (right), are a form of dwelling dating from prehistoric times. Made of shale rock, trulli are found only in the area of Apulia; the town shown is Alberobello. The flat sections of roof are used for drying walnuts in the sun as well as for hanging out the washing.

In the rest of the south, the land is mountainous, parched and poor. Olive oil rather than butter is the cooking medium — it costs less to keep an olive tree than a cow, and olive trees survive in poorer soil. Under the searing sun tempers run high, and the food is as fiery as those who eat it. Dried tubular pasta is served with angry sauces of garlic, hot peppers and burning chillies that take a little getting used to before their flavours can be truly appreciated.

The cooking of these poorer regions is largely based on pasta and vegetables, often cooked up together in a substantial soup. Fish soups of all kinds are made round the coast, but transport is difficult through the rocky terrain and fish is not often available inland. Instead, the locals keep chickens which scratch about in the streets, and make imaginative use of their hens' eggs, even combining them with sheeps' tripe in one dish.

Sicily and Sardinia

Sicily and Sardinia owe a lot of the distinctiveness of their cooking to the invaders from Greece, Phoenicia and Spain who have occupied the islands over the centuries. Both subsist mainly on a diet of pasta and bread, but Sicily produces early vegetables, olives and citrus fruit as well as wheat, while Sardinia is a pastoral island almost entirely devoted to rearing sheep and, to a lesser extent, goats.

From the Saracens, Sicily learned the art of making delicious sweets and pastries, among them cannoli, filled with cream cheese, chocolate and candied fruit, and cassata, a layered cake which includes the same ingredients, plus liqueur, and is covered in chocolate. Baking is a national pastime in Sicily. There are large loaves like cartwheels and savoury buns stuffed with pork, bacon and cheese.

Sardinians bake thin brittle circles of bread called carta di musica, music paper, and for weddings there are elaborately iced cakes inscribed with the names of the bride and groom. Sardinians are fond of roasting whole sheep and goats, as well as wild boar, suckling pig and smaller game, on an outdoor spit. Instead of using herbs, they build their fires of aromatic woods, such as juniper or olive, to give the barbecued meat its distinctive flavour.

The island of Sardinia gave its name to the sardine, which swims in its waters along with lobsters and eels — and all these foods are cooked as simply as they were thousands of years ago, by the Ancient Romans and before.

THE WINES OF SICILY AND SARDINIA

Sardinia's inhabitants are unlike mainland Italians, being more somber and reserved. Their wines are just as individual, many of them being as strong as sherry without being fortified. The whites are pinkish and the reds so dark as to be called vini neri — black wines.

Most of the wines of Sicily are strong and rough as in southernmost Italy, and most are produced in large co-operatives and used for blending. The one major exception is Marsala, the distinctive dessert wine very popular throughout Italy as well as abroad.

The production of Marsala was set up around 1760 by a Liverpudlian, John Woodhouse, who visited the island and realized that the wine produced there resembled the base wines of port, sherry and madeira.

The dry local white wine is fortified with wine brandy and sweetened with a local sweet wine made with part-dried grapes and unfermented grape juice, heated until it becomes syrupy.

Marsala is drunk as a dessert wine or an aperitif. It is also blended with egg yolks to make the rich, creamy dessert called zabaglione.

The Italian kitchen is homely and practical rather than sophisticated. Most of the equipment the Italian cook needs is basic and efficient, and essential to any working kitchen. Some of the ingredients too are those to be found in any well-stocked store cupboard, but the majority are redolent of the flavours and tastes unique to Italian cuisine.

THE ITALIAN KITCHEN

The first priority is a good set of sharp knives. There is nothing more frustrating or time-consuming than sawing away at a tough piece of meat or a squashy tomato with a blunt blade. A mezzaluna, a two-handled crescent-shaped knife with a wide blade, is excellent for chopping herbs, onions and garlic.

Choose a chopping board that does not have a join down the middle — the crack will only harbour food — and remember never to leave a wooden board to soak in water or it will warp.

You will need a large saucepan, preferably with a heavy bottom, for cooking pasta. It should hold 4 lt/2 pt water for 500 g/1 lb pasta, so that the pasta has room to boil without sticking. Stir it occasionally with a wooden spoon. A slotted spoon is useful for lifting out gnocchi as they cook and rise to the surface, and a colander is essential for draining.

Large ovenproof casseroles and small heavy-bottomed saucepans for making sauces will probably already be in your kitchen, as will that indispensable culinary tool, the cheese grater.

For making pasta, you do not need a pasta machine. Indeed, they can be extremely expensive and quite fiddly both to operate, and especially to clean. All you need is a large pastry board or a work surface that you can clean easily, a rolling pin, a pastry wheel and cutters, and a sharp knife.

*K*nives are of the utmost importance to the smooth functioning of an Italian kitchen. **1** large, sharp cook's knife; **2** vegetable paring knife; **3** decorative cutter with a corrugated edge; **4** fruit knife, **5** mezzaluna — a twin-handled, double-bladed chopper; **6** cleaver; **7** grapefruit knife.

*M*any modern Italian kitchens now boast a hand-turned pasta rolling and cutting machine (left). It ensures fine, even threads of tagliatelli and thin, smooth sheets of lasagne. A hand-held rotary cutter and a ravioli tray (above) are very useful for making meat, cheese, or vegetable-filled pastas.

A TREASURY OF INGREDIENTS

Get out of a train anywhere in Italy and a delicious smell will assail your nostrils and proclaim the identity of the city you have arrived in. In Venice, it's fish; in Naples, garlic; and in Bologna, butter. The store cupboard found in the average Italian kitchen similarly bursts with good things, most of them simple, very individual and highly aromatic.

ANCHOVIES

Anchovies are used in cooking all over Italy. You can buy anchovy fillets tinned in oil, anchovy paste and anchovy essence, but these are no real substitute for anchovies prepared at home. Whole salt-cured anchovies are sometimes available from Cypriot or Greek delicatessens, as well as specialist Italian shops. They are sold loose in a drum and should be filleted and steeped in oil as soon as possible.

Rinse the anchovies well in cold running water. Cover the work surface or a board with waxed paper, lay the fish on it and scrape off the skin. Remove the dorsal fin and the bones joined to it. Separate the fish into two halves with a knife and remove the spine. Lay the fillets in a shallow dish and cover each layer with olive oil. Make sure the top layer is completely submerged in oil. Store for up to two weeks in the fridge.

ALMONDS

Almonds were first brought to Italy by the Arabs and have been an essential ingredient in Italian cakes and pastries ever since.

To peel almonds, plunge them into boiling water. Remove the pan from the heat and leave the almonds in the water until the skins peel off easily. Alternatively, put the almonds in cold water, bring to the boil, drain and peel.

To toast peeled almonds, put them on a baking tray in a moderate oven. Turn frequently until they are golden brown.

Salted almonds may be served with drinks. Toast the almonds, dip them in lightly-beaten egg white and sprinkle with salt and cayenne, if liked. Return to a low oven to dry.

For sugared almonds, a favourite Italian sweet, shell but do not peel the almonds. Caramelize the same weight of sugar as you have almonds. Coat the almonds in the sugar and allow to set. Repeat the operation twice more, so that you have used three times as much sugar as almonds. Finally, dissolve a little gum arabic in water and dip the almonds in it. Spread them out on a wire mesh and leave to dry.

To grind almonds for use in cakes, puddings and pastries, peel the almonds and dry them in the oven without allowing them to brown. Pound them in a mortar with superfine sugar and sieve the resulting powder.

ANCHOVY BUTTER

Anchovy butter is a delicious spread for use in antipasti. Simply cream together 100g/4 oz buttter and 50g/2 oz anchovy paste.

BACCALÀ

Baccalà is cod preserved in salt. It is sold in drums and should be soaked for at least 24 hours in several changes of cold water before cooking.

ARTICHOKES

The artichoke is an edible thistle and has had a place of honour in kitchen gardens since the Renaissance. The Italians have a huge variety of artichoke recipes, including some for young artichokes eaten whole. Soak artichokes upside down in a bowl of cold water acidulated with vinegar or lemon juice. Cut off the stem near the base of the vegetable and cut the tips cleanly off the leaves. Rub any cut

edges with lemon juice.

Bring a large pan of salted, acidulated water to the boil. Put the artichokes in, stem down, bring back to the boil and test after 30 minutes to see if they are done. Tug at a leaf at the base of the largest artichoke — if it comes away easily, the artichokes are done. Drain them upside down in a colander.

Each diner will need a plate for the discarded leaves, a finger bowl and a large napkin. To eat, pull away the leaves,

beginning at the base. Dip the succulent base of the leaf in the sauce provided and nibble away the fleshy part. When all the leaves have been removed, discard the choke. Eat the delicious heart of the artichoke with a knife and fork and more of the sauce. To prepare artichokes for stuffing, slice off the top as well as the stem before you boil it.

When it is cooked, remove the inner leaves and the choke so that you are left with a cup.

If only the heart is needed, cook the artichokes in the usual way. Dismantle each artichoke, as if you were eating it, to uncover the heart.

BORLOTTI BEANS

Kidney-shaped beans eaten fresh and dried. They are very pretty, both pods and beans being speckled yellow, through pink to tawny brown. Tender, moist and sweet when cooked, they have a delicate and delicious flavour.

CAPERS

Capers are the small, green, unripe fruit of a climbing plant and have a very individual flavour. They are sold pickled in vinegar. If the vinegar is too strong, you may have to rinse the capers in water before use. Capers are much used in sauces for pasta, meat and fish.

Italy is famous for its coffees — black espresso and pale brown cappuccino, named after the colour of the monks' robes. Caffè alla Borgia is a popular mid-morning pick-me-up laced with apricot brandy and sprinkled with cinnamon. You can make Italian coffee at home in a napoletana - a coffee pot that has

a water jug inverted on top of it. Fill the water jug, spoon the ground coffee into the filter basket on top of it and fit the coffee pot, inverted, over that. Put the whole contraption on to heat and when the water boils, turn it upside down so that the water filters through the coffee into the pot beneath.

COFFEE

33

CHEESES

A salad of mozzarella and tomato, sprinkled with basil.

Parmesan is the best-known of all Italian cheeses. It accompanies pasta and rice and is ideal for cooking because it does not go stringy as it melts. It is also delicious at the end of a meal with fruit. If you can avoid it, never buy pre-grated parmesan sold in drums — it has no taste. Parmesan bought by the chunk should be pale yellow and finely honeycombed — the generic name for this cheese in Italy is grana, referring to its fine grain. The best grana is four years old and correspondingly expensive. Store large pieces of parmesan wrapped in two or three sheets of foil in the bottom of the fridge.

Bel paese is a creamy cheese from Lombardy, but with a very mild flavour. It can be used instead of mozzarella.

Fontina comes from Piedmont. It is a very fat, creamy cheese full of small holes and traditionally used to make fonduta, a non-alcoholic fondue.

Gorgonzola is a veined cows milk cheese from Lombardy. It has a strong flavour and a beautifully creamy texture. The greenish streaks are developed during maturation in caves or in aging rooms where the temperature and humidity of the caves is reproduced. Gorgonzola is often eaten creamed with butter and spread on bread.

Mascarpone is a small, double-cream cheese sold in a cheesecloth parcel and eaten with sugar and fruit.

Genuine mozzarella cheeses come from Campania and Apulia and are made with buffalo milk. True mozzarella is increasingly difficult to get hold of because of the scarcity of the buffalo. That commonly available today is made from cows milk. It should be eaten absolutely fresh and moist and is sold in round balls wrapped in waxed paper to keep it that way. If the cheese has dried out a little, it is best used in cooking or to top pizzas.

Pecorino is a sheeps milk cheese that can be used for cooking when mature. It has a piquant taste that increases with age and is produced in many regions of Italy including Tuscany, where it is delicate and creamy, and Sicily, where it can be smoked, salted, or flavoured with pepper or saffron.

Provola and provolone are also buffalo cheeses from Campania and come in different sizes and shapes. Tangier than mozzarella, they can be used in the same way. Cacio a cavallo is a similar cheese and gets its name from the way the cheeses are strung up in pairs 'astride' a rod to mature.

Ricotta is a moist curd cheese made from ewes milk and can be either mild or strong, according to region. In Piedmont and around Rome it is eaten very fresh with pepper and salt, or sometimes with coffee and sugar sprinkled on it. It can be used in cooking sweet and savoury dishes. In southern Italy Ricotta forte is made from salted ewes milk. It can be dried in the sun or in an oven and grated for cooking.

A selection of typical Italian cheeses; **1** *parmesan (grana);* **2** *pecorino;* **3** *fontina;* **4** *gorgonzola.*

FROGS

Frogs meat is very popular in Italy, especially in the north where an abundance of frogs is found in the rice fields. It has tender, delicate white flesh, which is easily digested and considered to be very good for invalids. It can be fried, with or without batter, or made into a delicious risotto.

GARNISHES FOR SOUPS

Soup is often a substantial dish in Italy and the garnishes are correspondingly hearty. Choose from pasta shapes, bread croûtons — fried or baked in the oven, and sometimes stuffed as well — or dumplings made of potato or semolina and mixed with spinach, chicken, ham or fish and béchamel sauce.

FUNGHI

In the autumn, Italians go mushroom hunting for porcini (ceps) which are very fleshy and can be served instead of a meat course. Strict laws govern the quantity and size of mushrooms a person may pick, and anyone finding a fungus of dubious species may have it checked by the authorities. Many different varieties of mushroom grow wild — the market at Trento sells 230 species. Mushrooms not eaten fresh can be dried for use during the rest of the year. Dried mushrooms should be soaked in warm water for a few minutes and not be cooked too long in a dish or they will lose their flavour.

CHICKPEAS

Chickpeas are often served in Italy with pasta (in a dish called tuoni e lampo — thunder and lightning) or in soups. The dried ones should be soaked for 48 hours and simmered for between two and six hours until tender. As this is a lengthy process, it may be wiser to buy the canned variety.

Ice cream originated in the Near East but today the world specialists in making ice cream are the Italians — especially the Neapolitans. The Italians were always partial to a cooling end to a meal — in Ancient Rome snow was brought down from the mountains and flavoured with crushed fruit.

In modern times the Italians became famous for their ice creams first in Paris, where the Neapolitan, Tortoni, created biscuit tortoni as well as a variety of gelati and granite in his ice cream parlour on the Boulevard des Italiens.

GELATI

GNOCCHI

These are dumplings made from semolina or potato. The singular, gnoccho, means thickhead or puddinghead, and gnocchi are a bit plain and stodgy on their own. They are usually eaten in a soup or with a sauce as an accompaniment to a meat dish. A very cheap and tasty meal is gnocchi baked in the oven with layers of cheese and tomato sauce. For recipes, see pp. 57 - 58.

The prince of herbs, basil.

HAZELNUTS

To peel hazelnuts, shell them and put them in a hot oven until the skin is charred. Rub them against a coarse metal colander to remove the skin.

HERBS

Wild herbs grow in profusion on Italian hillsides and have been used in Italian cooking at least since the days of Ancient Rome. Most popular are marjoram, sage, rosemary, thyme, parsley, bay and, of course, basil. Basil has a special affinity with tomatoes and, pounded with garlic, olive oil, parmesan and pine nuts, makes the wonderful Genoese speciality pesto, the most aromatic pasta sauce of all.

KID

Kid and sucking lamb (abbacchio) are great delicacies in Italy. They are also very expensive because they are slaughtered so young. At 4kg/9 lb they have tender white meat; at 10kg/22 lb it is a delicate pink. They should be eaten shortly after slaughter and not hung first.

MARINADES

A quick and delicious marinade for meat to be grilled can be made of oil and lemon juice, or from white wine mixed with chopped herbs and seasoned with salt and pepper. Add a dash of brandy, if you like it, and marinate steaks, chops and kebab pieces for an hour or two.

Marinate larger cuts of meat for several days (according to age and toughness) in a non-metallic bowl in the fridge. Turn it occasionally using a wooden spoon. For the marinade you will need a mixture of white wine and wine vinegar and a selection of chopped vegetables and parsley stems.

Alternatively, you can use a cooked marinade. Fry chopped vegetables gently in oil, add wine and vinegar, using a little more vinegar than you would in an uncooked marinade, and bring to the boil. Simmer for 30 minutes, allow to cool, then pour over the joint of meat.

POLENTA

Polenta has, in one form or another, been a staple Italian food for thousands of years. Today it is mainly made of yellow maize flour and often takes the place of bread in Lombardy and Veneto. The flour is boiled in water until it is stodgy, then poured onto a board and left to go cold, when it is cut into slices that are eaten cold, fried, or served with sauce. Recipes on p.59.

OLIVE OIL

Olive oil is one of the oldest and most popular culinary oils. The quality of the oil depends not on the quality of the olive but on its processing; the more refined the oil the lighter its colour and flavour. **1** pure olive oil which, although refined, retains some of its olive flavour and is widely used as a salad oil; **2** fine olive oil, refined further than pure olive oil, this type is not suitable for salads but is ideal for frying; **3** extra virgin olive oil is the best for salads. Taken from the first cold pressing of the olive, it is full of the flavour promised by its rich colour.

Olive oil is the major cooking medium around the Ligurian coast, in Tuscany and southern Italy. The best oil is said to come from Lucca in Tuscany. The first pressing of the olives produces a rich, fruity, green oil that is preferred by the cognoscenti to the mellower more golden variety produced later on. Sadly, oil for export is often blended for uniformity and much of its character is lost.

Buy the most expensive olive oil you can afford for use on salads and in cooking dishes where its strong flavour is a component part of the dish. Where the flavour would be obtrusive, substitute a cheaper tasteless oil such as peanut or arachide.
The best olive oil is too good and too expensive to be used indiscriminately.

PISTACHIO

Peel pistachio nuts by dropping them into boiling salted water for a few seconds; the salt helps the nuts keep their green colour. Remove the pan from the heat and leave the nuts to soak for a minute before peeling off the skins.

PINE NUTS

These come from the cones of the stone pine and are usually available from health food stores and delicatessens. They are small and creamy coloured with a sweet, delicate flavour. They are used in pesto and sweet and sour (agrodolce) sauces as well as in sweet cakes and biscuits.

PASTA

*T*aste in pasta divides Italy roughly into two. In the north of Italy and as far south as Rome the pasta is mainly of the ribbon variety — flat, fresh and home-made with egg. Around Naples and further south it is tubular, eggless, mass produced and dried.

Pasta for soups includes conchigliette (little shells), anellini (little hoops), nocchette (little bows) and semini (little seeds).

Pasta to be boiled includes fettucine (ribbons), fusilli (spirals), spaghetti, ziti (fat spaghetti), conchiglie (shells), penne (nibs), cappelletti (hats), farfalle (butterflies), macaroni and ruote (wheels).

Pasta to be stuffed includes lumache (snails), cannelloni, ravioli, and tortellini.

Instructions for making fresh pasta can be found on pp. 51-56.

First column, top to bottom:
1 *whole wheat bucatini*, **2** *creste*; **3** *lumaconi*; **4** *green bigoli*; **5** *lasagne*.

Second column, top to bottom:
6 *maccheroncini (frilled macaroni)*; **7** *sedanini*; **8** *vegetable macaroni*; **9** *long fusilli*; **10** *tagliatelli, fettucine*.

Third column, top to bottom:
11 semolina spaghetti; 12 lumachine; 13 marille; 14 viti; 15 zite.

Fourth column, top to bottom:
16 large macaroni; 17 elbow macaroni; 18 penne; 19 green viti; 20 reginelle; 21 pappardelle.

Fifth column, top to bottom:
22 whole wheat spaghetti; 23 farfalle; 24 canelloni; 25 trenitte; 26 thin pappardelle or mafaldine.

QUAIL

Quail is best in October. It does not need to be hung. Buy good fat ones. If you have a hearty appetite, allow two per person.

Sardines are known by many different names in Italy. The Italians say the sardine has 24 virtues and loses one every hour — therefore it should be eaten very fresh. To prepare fresh sardines, slit open the stomach and pull out the entrails and the backbone. Cut off the head, if preferred. Fresh sardines are delicious grilled over an open fire with a little rosemary, black pepper and lemon juice or dipped in flour, egg and breadcrumbs and fried.

RICE

Italy is Europe's biggest rice producer. Piedmont and Lombardy are the regions where it is grown. Italian rice has shorter, fatter, grains than the Asian variety. It takes a little longer to cook, but has more bite and body and is excellent for risotto and for soups where the grains must remain firm and creamy as well as succulent. Arborio is the variety usually exported. Asian rice is better for timbales, salads and pilaffs, because it can be cooked until it is dry and fluffy.

SAFFRON

Saffron gives its lovely colour to Milan's famous risotto. It comes from the pistils of the autumn-flowering crocus. Half a million pistils are needed to make about 2lb of saffron powder, thus it is very expensive.

SARDINES

This sharp green sauce is often served with boiled meats and with white fish. Use vinegar for a meat sauce and lemon juice for a fish one. Blend together 4 tablespoons olive oil and 1 tablespoon each of parsley and capers, 2 anchovy fillets, ½ clove of garlic and 1 teaspoon either red wine vinegar or lemon juice.

RADICCHIO

A speciality of Treviso, radicchio is shaped like a small round lettuce, but is rose-coloured with cream veins. Radicchio from Castelfranco has darker streaks against a lighter ground. Purists say the two should never be mixed.

SALSA VERDE

SAUSAGES AND COOKED MEATS

Each region of Italy has its special kind of salami. Sometimes the meat is fine ground, giving a smooth texture and a pale pink colour, or it may be coarse ground so that the sausage has large chunks of dark red and white meat, often dotted with black peppercorns.

Luganega is made from pork shoulder, parmesan and a little spice. A mild sausage with a high meat content, it is sold in continuous coils.

Mortadella is Italy's most famous sausage. It is made of different cuts of pork and comes from Bologna. Delicate in both taste and texture, it varies in size, sometimes reaching the astonishing girth of 18 inches.

Pancetta is the same cut of pork as bacon, but cured in salt and spices instead of being smoked. It is rolled into a sausage shape and sold sliced.

Parma ham, prosciutto, is made from the boned hind legs of the pig. It is first salted and then dried — the air in the hills around Parma being ideal to bring it to maturity. It is sliced paper thin. The tender, sweet, light red meat is popularly served as an appetizer with fresh figs or melon.

Zampone is a speciality of Modena — the boned foreleg of the pig stuffed with ground spiced pork. It is boiled and served sliced with other boiled meats.

Italian smoked and cured meats are delicious as antipasti or as cocktail snacks, and make exceptionally toothsome sandwiches. Above, top to bottom: prosciutto crudo — a delicate raw ham; 'Hungarian' salami; salt beef; pastrami — cured and smoked beef; a pale, marbled liver sausage; Milan salami; and mortadella — the fine-textured sausage of Bologna, often speckled with pistachio nuts.

SORBET

The Arabs brought the art of sorbet making to Italy. Sorbets are light ices made with fruit juice, wine or liqueurs (never cream or eggs) and are served as soon as they are frozen in tall glasses, perhaps with a trickle of wine or liqueur poured over. They used to be eaten between courses to refresh the palate, but are more common today as a dessert.

SEMOLINA

This is a flour — from coarse-ground durum wheat — used to make gnocchi. Durum wheat is also used in the manufacture of commercial pasta. Don't confuse it with the grain of the same name used to make a milk pudding.

TUNA

Tinned tuna, in oil or brine, is a useful item to have on hand for the delicious Tuscan salad of tonno e fagioli — tuna and white beans. Simply mix the two together with a little chopped onion and perhaps some parsley, and season with pepper.

SQUID

Squid comes from the cephalopod family, along with octopus and cuttlefish. To prepare it, pull the head gently away from the body. Discard the 'pen' and remove the pinkish purple skin from the body. Wash the body and cut it into rings. The fins are also edible. Cut off the tentacles and cut them into short lengths. Discard the head and the entrails.

SPICES

Spices have been used in Italian cooking since Roman times and during the Renaissance Venice was at the centre of the spice trade between the Far East and Europe.

Nutmeg is used in savoury and sweet dishes that contain spinach or ricotta. Cloves are found in the rich panforte of Siena, vanilla sugar in sweet pastries and creams.

STOCKFISH

This is wind-dried cod and should not be confused with baccalà, salt cod. Stockfish (from the Norwegian stock, for stick, as it is dried wound around poles) is sold hanging up in the shop. Beat the stockfish with a pestle to break down the fibres and soak it until tender enough to cook. As preparation is so lengthy, it is not surprising that this fish is not widely available and can only be bought in speciality shops.

Though an indispensable ingredient in Italian cooking, the tomato was introduced into the country only comparatively recently. The Italians grow either plum tomatoes or the huge, curved, irregular Marmande variety — both have infinitely more flavour than the pale, insipid specimens cultivated elsewhere. Many Italians bottle their own tomatoes and make their own tomato concentrate at home for use during the winter months. Those who have neither the time nor the space use the tinned variety, as we do. (There are recipes for home-made tomato sauce on pp. 45-47).

Truffles grow in Tuscany, Romagna and Piedmont and are hunted by dogs specially trained to sniff them out during the truffle season, which runs from October to March. They are eaten raw, sliced on risotto or fonduta, or cooked in butter and served under a mound of freshly grated parmesan.

TRUFFLES

TOMATO

OFFAL

All kinds of offal meats are popular in Italy, including calves head, pigs feet, tripe, tongue and lung. Calves brains and sweetbreads (the thymus gland) are especially prized delicacies. Brains should be washed thoroughly under the cold tap, then soaked in cold water for ten minutes. Drain, and remove the blood vessels and membranes. Simmer for about 20 minutes in salted acidulated water to which you have added some carrot, onion and celery, then drain and allow to cool.

Refrigerate until firm. Slice the brains thickly, dip in egg and then in breadcrumbs and fry briefly in oil over a high heat until golden. Drain on kitchen paper and serve with lemon wedges.

Italians do not feel it necessary to soak sweetbreads for hours in several changes of water until all the blood has disappeared. They should be washed under cold running water, when most of the membrane can be removed. They can then be cooked as for brains, above.

Vitello is meat from a milk-fed calf slaughtered at three weeks. Vitellone is meat from an older, grass-fed, non-working animal. Beef comes from a working animal, the ox (manzo) and not from the cow (mucha). To make perfect scaloppine you need good veal cut into thin slices across the grain. Then the scaloppine should be pounded to make them thinner and flatter. The idea is not to hammer at them indiscriminately, but to bring the pounder down and slide it forward at the same time, stretching the meat. Turn the meat as you go and stretch it evenly all around.

VEAL

BASIC
RECIPES

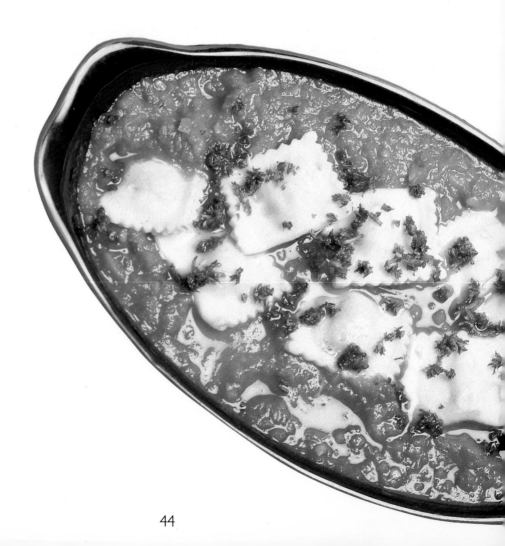

SALSA DI POMODORO

Basic tomato sauce

Ingredients/makes 4 large jars	
7kg/14 lb good-quality ripe tomatoes	1 small head of garlic
	8 cloves
1kg/2 lb medium onions	Salt
1kg/2 lb tender carrots	Olive oil
400g/14 oz green celery	2 teaspoons salicylic acid (from a chemist)
3/4 cup parsley, sage and basil, mixed	

T his sauce will keep in wide-topped airtight jars for a year or more. You can leave out salicylic acid if you sterilize the jars and the contents (see below). Use the sauce to flavour soups and as a base for other sauces, or just heat it up and use on its own. □ □ Wash the tomatoes well and cut them up roughly, removing the stalk and any seeds. Put in a large pan, preferably stainless steel or heavy aluminium. Prepare, wash and coarsely chop the onions, carrots, celery and herbs. Add to the pan. Peel the garlic and add the cloves to the pan. □ □ Heat gently, and as soon as it starts to simmer, lower the heat, cover and cook for 2½ hours, stirring occasionally. If the tomatoes are very watery, drain after 30 minutes and continue to cook. □ □ Do not let any condensed water from the lid drop into the sauce when you lift the lid. Make sure the sauce does not stick to the pan, and put an asbestos mat under it if necessary. □ □ When the sauce is cooked, press it through a strainer into a large pan and lightly salt it. Add a glass of olive oil and cook for a further hour. Let it cool and add ¼ teaspoon salicylic acid for every 1kg/2 lb of sauce by putting a ladleful of sauce into a bowl, adding the acid, then returning the sauce to the pan and stirring in well. Let the sauce cool completely. □ □ Wash and dry jars and fill with cold sauce. Occasionally bang the jars onto a folded cloth so that the contents settle and no air is left in the jars. Finally, clean the opening of the jars to prevent mould from growing. Leave the jars uncovered for a day, then pour on 50mm/¼ inch oil, seal and store. Some people pour the boiling sauce into jars without adding salicylic acid and seal them tightly. They find that the sauce keeps just as well.

Ravioli makes a mouthwatering first course, whether served steaming hot in a cooked tomato sauce or chilled in a thick salsa of strained and herbed fresh tomato pulp.

SALSA DI POMODORO PICCANTE
Piquant tomato sauce

Makes 6lt/9 pt	1 bay leaf
1.3kg/2¾ lb firm ripe tomatoes	Salt
4 medium firm peppers	300ml/½ pt good quality white
1 pickled red pepper	wine vinegar
1 small red paprika pepper	2 tablespoons sugar
200g/7 oz sliced onions	½ teaspoon salicylic acid
2 cloves	(from a chemist)
1 stick of cinnamon	Olive oil

T his sauce is similar to tomato ketchup and makes a good accompaniment to roast and boiled meats and hard-boiled eggs. Wash and remove stalks from the tomatoes, cut in half and deseed, and put in a large pan (not an aluminium one). Wash the peppers, dry, halve, deseed and remove the pith. Add to the tomatoes. □ □ Add the pickled pepper, a piece of paprika, the onion, cloves, cinnamon stick, bay leaf and 1 teaspoon salt. Stir well and simmer for 3 hours on a very low heat. □ □ Make sure condensation on the pan lid does not drip into the sauce. Use a cloth or absorbent paper to mop it up when you lift the lid. □ □ When the cooking time is up, remove the pan from the heat and sieve the mixture, discarding cloves, bay leaf and cinnamon. Return the purée to the pan, add the vinegar and sugar and simmer on a very low heat for about 2 hours. □ □ Now weigh a dish and pour the cooked sauce into it. Weigh again and subtract the weight of the dish so that you have the exact weight of your sauce (you should have about 1 kg/2 lb). Let it cool. Put a few tablespoons into a cup and add ¼ teaspoon acid for each 1 kg/2 lb of sauce. Stir well, then mix carefully into the sauce so that it is evenly distributed. □ □ Pour the sauce into small jars (that can be put directly onto the table) or into bottles. Clean the necks of the containers and leave to stand until the next day. Finally pour a good 1 cm/½ inch of oil on top of the sauce, seal the jars hermetically and store in a cupboard. □ □ If you do not want to use salicylic acid, sterilize the jars when you have poured sauce into them.

SALSA DI POMODORO CON CARNE
Tomato and meat sauce

Makes about 4.5kg/9lb sauce	75g/3 oz butter
4kg/8 lb firm ripe tomatoes	½ glass olive oil
2kg/1 lb tender carrots	1kg/2 lb ground lean minced beef
200g/7 oz green celery	
125g/5 oz parsley, sage and basil	About 1 teaspoon salicylic acid (from a chemist)
5 cloves of garlic, crushed	Salt
500g/1 lb thinly sliced onions	

P repare the tomato sauce as before, but without the onions. Put the onions in a pan with the butter and olive oil. Heat gently, until softened, add the meat and cook for 1½ hours, adding a little tomato juice if necessary. Combine the meat sauce with the tomato sauce and cook for a further hour, then allow to cool until tepid. Add ¼ teaspoon salicylic acid for each 1kg/2 lb sauce. Just reheat for serving with pasta.

Each serving of spaghetti should be topped with just enough sauce to flavour and moisten it, but the texture of the pasta should predominate.

BAGNA CAUDA
Hot anchovy dip

Ingredients/serves 4	25g/1 oz fresh butter
100g/4 oz anchovies in brine	200ml/⅓pt virgin olive oil
5 cloves of garlic	Salt

B agna cauda is a hot dip, a speciality of Piedmont. It is brought to the table in a terracotta saucepan and put over a little candle — if possible each person should have their own chafing dish. Each person dips crudités or cooked vegetables into the sauce. These are tender white cardoons — a relation of the thistle and the artichoke — soaked first in acidulated cold water; peppers, celery, tender cauliflower florets, or cooked onions, potatoes, beets, carrots and turnips, etc. ☐ ☐ Make sure the bagna cauda dish is stable to avoid accidents. If you want the garlic to be more digestible, soak it for 2 hours before use in a glass of milk. In some parts of Piedmont it is customary to add crushed pieces of walnut to the dip. Leftovers of the sauce can be served with scrambled eggs. ☐ ☐ Wash, fillet and dry the anchovies well. Cut the garlic into fine slivers or, if preferred, peel and crush it. Put the terracotta pan over a low flame and add the butter and garlic. Let it cook gently for a few minutes without browning, then gradually add the oil and anchovies. Blend the anchovies in well and cook over a very low flame for about 15 minutes, stirring occasionally. Finally taste and add salt, if necessary. Serve in the cooking dish.

PESTO ALLA GENOVESE
Basil and garlic sauce

Ingredients/serves 4	1 teaspoon pinenuts or a well
About 30 leaves of freshly	peeled walnut kernel
picked basil	1 tablespoon grated parmesan
Salt	cheese
3 cloves of garlic, peeled	Virgin olive oil

T he Ligurians say that the basil should be grown in Liguria! If possible, use the top leaves of the basil plant. ☐ ☐ Gently wash the basil leaves and pat as dry as possible; put them in a mortar (a marble one for preference), add a pinch of salt (to help the basil retain its vivid green colour), the garlic, pine nuts or walnut (make sure it does not taste rancid).

□ □ Crush all the ingredients with a pestle, gradually adding parmesan (this will prevent the paste slipping out of the mortar) and pecorino. If you prefer, use extra parmesan instead of the pecorino and another table-spoon of olive oil. □ □ When you have a smooth paste, add 2-3 tablespoons olive oil, mixing well with a wooden spoon. □ □ The pesto is then ready to serve. When using pesto to flavour pasta, dilute it first with a spoonful of pasta cooking water or a nut of cold butter to thin it a little. If it is to be used to flavour minestrone, dilute it with a spoonful of soup and then add to the minestrone just before taking it from the heat.

*F*resh basil provides a brilliant green colour and an inimitable flavour. If it is not available, parsley will provide a green sauce with quite a different emphasis.

PASTA

A 500g/1lb packet of dried pasta will serve five people. Bring 4lt/7pt water to the boil in a large saucepan. Add a pinch of salt and about 1 teaspoon oil. Add the pasta and turn up the heat to get the water back to boiling point as quickly as possible. Cook it at a full rolling boil, stirring occasionally with a wooden spoon, for about 10 minutes. Remember that pasta continues to cook for a few moments when you take it off the heat, so allow for this by stopping when the pasta is just al dente. When it is ready, add a measure of cold water to stop cooking and then drain. Meticulous draining is not necessary, as pasta should not dry out. (Italians say pasta is greedy for water.) The process is exactly the same for fresh pasta, but you will need about 250g/8oz pasta per person, and the cooking time will be only about 4 minutes.

Using a pasta machine

The dough should be firmer than for hand-rolled pasta. Feed the dough into the machine in small pieces, each rolled in flour, then it will not be so likely to stick to the blades.

PASTA FATTA IN CASA
Homemade pasta

Ingredients/serves 4	4 medium eggs
400g/14oz flour (make sure it's not stale)	Oil

F or pasta to be cooked in soup, make half this quantity. Dust the board or working surface with flour. Spread the flour (which should be as fresh as possible)onto the board and make a well in the centre. Break the eggs into it. (Any shell will ruin the pasta.) Add 1 tablespoon cold water to the eggs and 1 or 2 teaspoons oil. Beat the eggs with a fork and gradually work in the flour, using your hands when the dough becomes stiff. Knead for at least 10 minutes. The dough should be stiff — add extra flour if it is too soft. When little air bubbles start to appear, roll the dough into a ball, flatten it and then roll it out with a rolling pin as far as possible, making sure that the thickness is uniform.

Step-by-step below

Make a well in the mound of flour, break in the eggs and beat with a fork. **1**

2 Gradually work in flour. When the dough stiffens, carry on using your hands.

Knead vigorously for at least 10 minutes. **3**

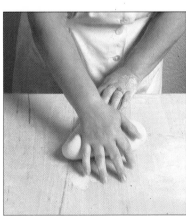

4 When bubbles appear, roll the dough into a ball and then flatten it.

Continued over page

Roll out with a rolling pin. Starting from the centre, roll out in all directions. **5**

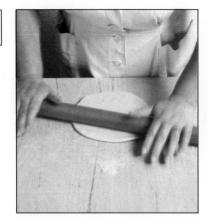

6 **Turn dough round, using a rolling pin.**

Put it back down on the board and continue to roll out in the other direction. **7**

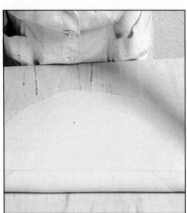

PASTA ROSSA
Red pasta

Ingredients/serves 4	1 teaspoon tomato paste
400g/14 oz flour	3 eggs
250g/8 oz tender carrots	Salt

T he amount of flour used here will vary according to the moisture content of the vegetables. Steam the carrots and press through a fine strainer into a pan. Put it onto heat and stir with a wooden spoon to dry out the pureé. Stir in the tomato paste and let it cool. Proceed as with egg pasta, adding more flour if necessary. Add the carrot mixture to the eggs in the flour well. ☐ ☐ This pasta, like the spinach variety, does not roll out as thinly as basic pasta dough. Treat it like plain egg pasta. Using three colours of pasta, you can prepare harlequin pasta.

PASTA VERDE
Green pasta

Ingredients/serves 4	400g/14oz flour
200g/7 oz raw spinach	3 eggs

Wash the spinach, discarding tough stalks and discoloured leaves. Cook it in only the water clinging to it, squeeze out the water and work through the strainer or use a blender. Make the dough as usual, add the spinach and knead for 10 minutes. If the dough is too soft, add a little more flour. It is difficult to stretch out green pasta very thinly.

TAGLIATELLE

Tagliatelle is the simplest pasta shape to make — therefore it is probably the most commonly found. Make the pasta — white, red or green — as directed in the preceding pages. Roll it out as thinly as possible, then beginning at one end, roll the dough into a long, thin cylinder. Beginning at one end, cut the roll into slices, rather like cutting a Swiss roll. Gently ease the slices into separate strands of tagliatelle.

Step-by-step below

Using a knife with a wide blade, cut roll into slices of desired thickness. **1**

2 Separate and spread out pasta shapes on board.

AGNOLINI

P roceed as for tagliatelle, making the dough a little firmer as it is to be rolled out more thinly. Cut squares 2.5cm/1 inch wide for serving in soup, otherwise 5cm/2 inches wide. Fill generously with stuffing and fold the pasta over. Put your index finger against the side of the pasta envelope and curve the pasta, joining the two ends. There should be a little hole in the centre of the agnolino. *Step-by-step 1-3 below*

Cut pasta into strips 1 inch wide and place strips on top of one another. **1**

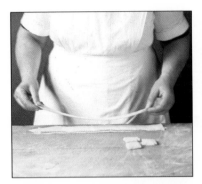

2 Using a sharp knife, cut strips into squares.

Put your index finger against side where the pasta was folded and turn two ends round your finger. **3**

1 To make cappelletti, use your hands and not the board.

CAPPELLETTI

I t is thought this pasta shape got its name from the alpine hats it resembles. Prepare pasta as for tagliatelle, and let it rest under a cloth. Using a little serrated cutter or a sharp knife, cut pasta into squares with 1-1½ inch long sides. Place a pea-sized amount of filling in the middle of each square, then fold into a triangle, joining the two ends. Then, keeping left index finger under filling, join the two points of the triangle, making sure that there is no hole (unlike agnolini). Stretch widthways a little, if necessary. *Step 1 above*

CAPPELLETTI TOSCANI

Prepare the pasta with a little less egg (3 eggs to 400g/14 oz flour). When the dough has been rolled out, cut out circles, using a wine glass. Put meat filling in the centre of each circle. Fold over one half of the circle to make a semicircle. Holding the shape in your hands (not on the board) press the edges round the filling, then join the two points of the half-moon shape. Do not turn the pasta round the filling but leave it as it is, as though it were the brim of a little hat. There should be a small hole in the centre.   *Step-by-step below*

1 Cut out circles on rolled out dough, place meat filling on top, and fold in half.

2 Close edges around filling and press seal flat. Join corners of half circles together.

ANOLINI

These are a Bolognese specialty. Roll out dough and, using a glass with a sharp rim about 5cm/2 inches in diameter, cut out circles. Fill with a nut-sized piece of meat filling and fold over the free pasta, making a little rim on the lower semicircle. Press the rim round the filling and then, as for agnolini, shape the pasta round your left index finger.

RAVIOLI

These are common to all parts of Italy. They can be made with plain or egg pasta and are much like tortellini (see over page). Make them square or round.

TORTELLINI AND TORTELLONI

Prepare the pasta as before and roll out. Cover the pasta with a damp cloth to avoid drying out, except in the area where you are working. There are two basic tortellini shapes: square — like ravioli — and curved triangles with the edges joined. When these are large and served as a first course in a sauce instead of in a broth, they are often called tortelloni. Both plain and green tortellini/tortelloni are popular. Below is a simple version of tortelloni verde al gratin. *Step-by-step below*

Place a nut-sized piece of filling — either meat or ricotta and spinach — towards one corner of a square of pasta.

1

2 Fold the top over to form a triangle and join the points together to make a curved shape.

Place the tortelloni in a shallow dish and cover with a quantity of homemade tomato sauce.

3

4 Cover with a thick layer of mozzarella cheese. Cook for 45 minutes until bubbling, then serve.

GNOCCHI DI PATATE
Potato dumplings

First recipe/serves 4	Second recipe/serves 4
600g/1¼ lb floury white potatoes	500g/1 lb floury white potatoes
1 teaspoon salt	1 teaspoon salt
1 tablespoon grappa	2 eggs
1 egg	300g/10 oz flour
250g/8 oz flour	

T hese gnocchi can be served with butter and parmesan, sage butter or tomato sauce, meat sauce or pesto. ☐ ☐ Peel the potatoes and boil them in salted water over a low heat. Use even-sized potatoes, so they cook evenly. When just tender, drain, and while still hot mash and put the purée onto a board. Make a well in the middle of the purée and put in the salt, grappa if using, and egg (or eggs). ☐ ☐ Then pour on the flour and mix well to give a firm dough that does not stick to your hands. The amount of flour will vary depending on how moist the potato purée is. Knead the dough for some minutes. Cut off a piece of dough and roll into a sausage on a floured board. Cut off 2.5cm/1 inch slices, roll into balls and flour well. Take a grater (or fork) and decorate the dumplings with holes or ridges, pressing in with your finger on one side to give a shell shape. ☐ ☐ Put a large pan of salted water on to boil and gently put in all the gnocchi at once. When they come to the surface and float, remove them with a slotted spoon, keeping the water boiling, and put in a casserole dish. Pour over hot sauce of your choice, sprinkle with parmesan, add a second layer of gnocchi etc. Put a cover on the dish and place over a saucepan of boiling water to let the gnocchi absorb the flavour of the sauce. *Step-by-step below*

Mash potato, mix in other ingredients and blend well. | **1**

2 | Cut dough into pieces, rolling out each one by hand.

Continued over page

Continued from previous page

Cut each piece into thick discs, flour and mark with fork prongs on one side. **3**

4 They can also be pressed against the reverse side of a grater.

GNOCCHI DI SEMOLINA

Pour the cooked semolina onto a wide dish or onto a marble slab which has been lightly oiled. **1**

2 With a metal spatula spread to about ½ inch thickness.

With a dough cutter or glass, cut dough into discs. **3**

4 Lift up gnocchi and lay in a buttered dish.

Both semolina and potato gnocchi are favorites of northern Italy. They are particularly popular as a dish for meatless holy days and Fridays.

Gnocchi di Semolina
Semolina dumplings

Ingredients/serves 4	6 tablespoons parmesan cheese
750ml/1¼pt milk	2 egg yolks
Salt and pepper	Pinch of nutmeg
200g/7oz fine semolina	Breadcrumbs
100g/4oz butter	

T hese are sometimes thought to be a Roman speciality, but in fact they are eaten all over Italy. □ □ Heat the milk with a pinch of salt, and when it boils, gradually add the semolina, stirring the whole time with a wooden spoon to avoid lumps. Continue to cook, stirring, for 20 minutes. □ □ Remove from the heat and add 25g/1oz butter in small pieces. Then gradually stir in 2 tablespoons parmesan cheese, the egg yolks, one at a time, a pinch of pepper and nutmeg. □ □ Oil 1 or 2 large dishes or a clean marble kitchen slab and pour the semolina mixture on. Spread out to 1cm/½ inch thickness using a cold wet spatula and allow to cool. □ □ Preheat the oven to 180°C350°F/Gas 4. Melt a little butter and grease a casserole dish. □ □ Cut out squares or circles of semolina dough and place in the casserole. Assemble the dish in layers of gnocchi, melted butter and parmesan cheese. Sprinkle breadcrumbs over and put the dish in the oven for about 20 minutes or until golden brown.

Step-by-step, page 58

Polenta

P olenta can be made either from finely-ground maize meal, coarser yellow flour or from buckwheat flour. □ □ The best pan for polenta is a copper one (not tinned) with a convex bottom to make stirring easier. Polenta should be cooked in the proportion of 1½ cups polenta flour to 6¼ cups salted water, and this should not come more than halfway up the saucepan. The quantities vary according to how it is to be served. If a sauce is to be served with it, for four people you will need 3½ cups polenta flour, and 11¼ cups water. □ □ For coarse meal, boil the water, then add the meal gradually in handfuls, stirring to avoid lumps. The cooking time will vary from 40 minutes to about an hour. Stir the mixture continuously, scraping the sides and bottom of the pan. □ □ When

Continued over page

Continued from previous page

the polenta comes away easily from the sides of the pan at the end of cooking time, loosen it with a slotted spoon moistened in cold water, and turn it out. Serve the polenta very hot. ☐ ☐ If you use finer polenta meal, add a fifth of it to the cold water before putting it on to boil, then cover the pot and bring to the boil. Boil for 10 minutes, then gradually add the rest and proceed as before.

PASTA PER PIZZA
Pizza dough

Ingredients/serves 4	100g/4oz flour
25g/1oz fresh yeast	Pinch of salt

C rumble the yeast into a cup and dissolve it in a little tepid water (not too hot or it will prevent rising). Mix in about 25g/1oz flour, cover the cup with a cloth and leave in a warm place to rise. ☐ ☐ Put the remaining flour onto a board, add a pinch of salt, and make a well in the middle. Add the yeast mixture and work in gradually, adding just enough tepid water to make the dough smooth and pliable. ☐ ☐ Knead for a few minutes, then roll the dough into a ball, put in a floured bowl, cover with a cloth and put in a warm place until the dough has doubled in volume. ☐ ☐ Once risen, the dough is ready to be made into pizzas. ☐ ☐ For homemade pizza you can buy ready-made bread dough, to which you just need to add 1 tablespoon oil, knead and roll out. This is a much quicker method than making pizza dough from scratch. For a small pizza it is better to buy ready-made dough; for a large one it is cheaper to make your own.

Step-by-step below

1 Measure the fresh or dried yeast and the flour carefully. Sieve the flour into a large bowl.

2 Make a well in the center of the flour and pour in the yeast mixture and a little tepid water.

Using a **3** palette knife or spatula, mix until you have a firm, plastic dough. If extra water is required, work in carefully to avoid dough becoming sticky.

Turn **4** dough out onto a floured board and knead vigorously for 10 minutes.

Place the **5** dough in a lightly floured bowl. Cover with plastic wrap. Put in a warm place and allow to double in volume.

Turn the **6** risen dough onto a floured board. Knead and punch back until all air pockets are eliminated. The dough should be smooth, firm and elastic.

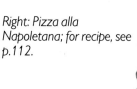

Right: Pizza alla Napoletana; for recipe, see p.112.

ANTI PASTI

Antipasti are savoury morsels designed to whet the appetite. Serve an attractive arrangement of eggs, olives, pickled vegetables, artichoke hearts, asparagus, and anchovies, or paper-thin slices of prosciutto with melon or figs, or choose from any of the following recipes.

MOUSSE DI POMODORO IN GELATINA
Jellied tomato mousse

Ingredients/serves 4	200ml/⅓pt thick béchamel sauce
500g/1lb skinned, deseeded and chopped tomatoes	Small carton cream, whipped
	1 sachet instant gelatine
Salt	Sherry

LAZIO, UMBRIA
AND
THE MARCHES

Blend or press the tomato flesh through a strainer, season with salt and cook gently for 5 minutes. Put to drain in a cloth tied up at 4 corners over a bowl for 2½ hours. Mix thoroughly with the béchamel sauce, press through a strainer or blend — and then pour into a bowl. Refrigerate for 20 minutes. ☐ ☐ Mix with a wooden spoon to give a soft, smooth consistency. Fold in the whipped cream. ☐ ☐ Prepare the gelatine according to the instructions on the packet and flavour with sherry. Pour half the gelatine into a glass bowl, and swirl it round to cover the sides. Let it set. Keep the remaining gelatine warm to prevent it from setting. Fill the bowl with the tomato mixture and pour over the remaining gelatine. Chill until set. Invert onto a serving dish, turn out and serve. *Photograph page 66*

POMODORI ALLA SICILIANA
Baked stuffed tomatoes

Ingredients/serves 4	3 tablespoons capers
8 large ripe tomatoes	2 tablespoons breadcrumbs
1 onion, finely chopped	4 tablespoons pitted and sliced ripe olives
Oil	
8 anchovy fillets, de-salted and pounded to a paste	Nutmeg (optional)
	Salt and pepper
1 bunch of parsley, chopped	

SICILY

Preheat the oven to 180°C/350°F/Gas 4. Cut the tops off the tomatoes and reserve. Scoop out the flesh and de-seed it, turn the tomatoes over and drain. Fry the onion in a little oil, add the anchovies, parsley, capers, breadcrumbs and olives. Season with salt, pepper and a little nutmeg, if liked, and mix well. Divide the mixture between the tomatoes and stuff them. Cap with the reserved lids. Put the tomatoes in an ovenproof dish, trickle oil over them and bake for 30 minutes. *Photograph page 67*

CHIZZE CON FORMAGGIO ALL'EMILIANA
Parmesan cheese fritters

EMILIA-ROMAGNA

Ingredients/serves 4	100g/4 oz fresh parmesan in
500g/1lb flour	one piece
Salt	Oil or lard for frying
200g/7 oz butter or lard,	Parsley
slightly softened and diced	Pinch of baking powder

Cut the parmesan into thin slivers, or grate coarsely. Pour the flour, baking powder and 1 tablespoon salt onto a board. Make a well in the centre and add 150g/5 oz butter. Rub it into the flour and add enough lukewarm water to form a dough. Knead for 10 minutes and roll out to a thin rectangular sheet. □ □ 5cm/2 inches in from the edge of the pastry, arrange little heaps of cheese at intervals in a row. Dot each pile of cheese with butter. Fold the pastry over the cheese and press well down with your fingers. With a pastry cutter or a knife, cut off the filled strip and cut round each mound of cheese, making sure the edges are well sealed into squares or oblongs. □ □ Continue until all the pastry is used up. Fry the parcels in plenty of hot oil or lard. Remove when golden brown and puffed up and drain on paper towels. Arrange on a serving dish, garnish with parsley and serve very hot.

SFORMATO DI FORMAGGIO
Cheese soufflé mould

EMILIA-ROMAGNA

Ingredients/serves 4	100g/4 oz sliced gruyère
100g/4 oz butter	cheese
100g/4 oz flour	100g/4 oz grated parmesan cheese
600ml/1 pt hot milk	Salt and pepper
	4 eggs, separated

Preheat the oven to 200°C/400°F/Gas 6. Melt the butter and gradually stir in the flour. Remove from the heat and gradually pour on the hot milk, still stirring, to prevent lumps forming. Stir in the cheeses, season and remove from the heat. Pour into a bowl and allow to cool. Add the egg yolks to the sauce. Beat the egg whites until peaks form when the whisk is removed. □ □ Pour the sauce into a greased and floured mould and fold in the egg whites. Cook in a bain marie in the oven until set (about 30 minutes). Remove from the oven and allow to stand for a few minutes before turning out onto a dish. Serve at once.

MOZZARELLA IN CAROZZA
Mozzarella in carriages

Ingredients/serves 4	Flour
1 large mozzarella	2 eggs
10 square slices white bread, trimmed	1-2 tablespoons cream or milk
	Salt

CAMPANIA

Drain the mozzarella if very wet, then cut into thin slices and cover half the slices with cheese. Press the remaining bread on top. Pour cold water into a bowl and put a little flour into a second bowl. Dip each sandwich first in the flour, then in the water, holding the edges firmly, and arrange the sandwiches on the bottom of a large dish. Break the eggs into a cup, beat with the milk or cream and pour over the sandwiches. Let them stand for 10 minutes. Turn the sandwiches over to coat completely with the egg mixture. Heat some oil or butter in a frying pan and brown the sandwiches on both sides. Serve very hot.

SARDINE SOTT'OLIO ALLA VENETA
Sardines with pepper and tomato sauce

Ingredients/serves 4	350g/12 oz skinned, deseeded and chopped tomatoes
12 sardines in oil	25g/1 oz butter
1 green or red pepper, baked, skinned and cut into strips	A few sage leaves, chopped
White of 3 hard-boiled eggs, chopped	1 clove of garlic, crushed
	Salt and pepper

VENETO

Bone the sardines carefully and reassemble them on a serving dish. Decorate with the pepper and egg white. Press the tomato flesh through a strainer and cream with the butter, sage and garlic. Season the sauce and spoon over the sardines. *Photograph page 71*

MOUSSE DI POMODORO IN GELATINA

*J*ELLIED TOMATO MOUSSE
For recipe, see p.63

POMODORI ALLA SICILIANA

***B*AKED STUFFED TOMATOES**
For recipe, see p.63

PROSCIUTTO COTTO IN GELATINA
Cooked ham in gelatine

*EMILIA-
ROMAGNA*

Ingredients/serves 4	I sachet instant gelatine
8 slices cooked ham	Sherry

Cut the ham slices in half and roll them up. Prepare the gelatine according to the instructions on the packet and flavour with a small glass of sherry. Pour a little gelatine into the bottom of a dish and refrigerate. When set, arrange the ham rolls on it, trickle over the remaining gelatine and chill for 2 hours. The ham rolls may also be stuffed with pâté or Russian salad.   *Photograph page 71*

PATE DI CONIGLIO
Rabbit pâté

*LAZIO, UMBRIA
AND
THE MARCHES*

Ingredients/serves 12	I glass marsala
I rabbit weighing 2kg/4½lb	I glass brandy
100g/4 oz butter	I sachet instant gelatine
4 tablespoons oil	I small black truffle (optional)
I clove of garlic	Pickled vegetables, such
A sprig of rosemary	as cauliflower, peppers, etc,
Salt and freshly ground pepper	to decorate
I glass dry white wine	

Wash and joint the rabbit, reserving liver. Put the rabbit in a pan with 25g/1 oz butter, the oil, garlic and rosemary. Season and cook over a low heat until the joints are browned all over. Pour in the wine and let it evaporate a little. Turn down the heat. Cook for an hour, adding a little hot water, if necessary. Add the liver 5 minutes before you take the rabbit off the heat. ☐ ☐ Drain and bone the rabbit joints. Chop the meat and press it through a fine-meshed strainer or put it in a blender until you have a smooth, even paste. Transfer to a bowl. Add the remaining butter, melted, and mix with a wooden spoon. Add the marsala and brandy, sprinkle with a little freshly ground pepper and mix well. Prepare the gelatine according to the instructions on the packet and pour a little into a rectangular mould, tipping it to coat. Put in the refrigerator to set. ☐ ☐ Cut the truffle, if using, and the pickled vegetables with a shape cutter and arrange the decoration on the sides and bottom of the mould. Cover with another layer of gelatine and put in the refrigerator to chill and set. Cover with a further layer of gelatine. Put the mould back in the refrigerator. You should now have a thickish coating of gelatine. ☐ ☐ When the gelatine has set, fill the mould with the rabbit mixture, leaving a small gap between the sides and the pâté. Smooth the top down well. Pour the remaining gelatine into the mould, letting it completely fill the gaps at the sides and cover the top, and leave to chill for 3-4 hours. Turn the pâté onto a serving dish and allow it to stand for 30 minutes before serving.

SUPPLI ALLA ROMANA
Roman rice croquettes

Ingredients/serves 4	A few dried mushrooms
I small onion, sliced	Olive oil
100g/4 oz butter	100g/4 oz lean minced veal
50g/2 oz skinned and sliced sausage	Tomato paste
	Meat extract
300g/10 oz peeled, deseeded and chopped ripe tomatoes	Salt
	2 finely chopped chicken livers
350g/12 oz rice	100g/4 oz diced mozzarella cheese
1lt/2 pt stock	Breadcrumbs
2 eggs, beaten	Oil or lard for deep-frying

LAZIO, UMBRIA AND THE MARCHES

L eftovers can be used to make this economical dish. Reserving a little onion, put the rest into a pan with some butter and the sausage and fry for a few minutes. Add the tomatoes and cook gently for 10 minutes, stirring frequently. Add the rice and pour in a ladleful of stock, adding another each time it is absorbed by the rice. When cooked, remove from the heat and add 25g/1 oz butter and the eggs and mix well. Then turn onto a plate and cool. ☐ ☐ Meanwhile, soak the mushrooms, drain and slice. Chop the reserved onion slices and put in a saucepan with a little butter and oil. Then add the mushrooms and veal. Dilute the tomato paste and a little meat extract in a few tablespoons of water and add to the pan. Season to taste and cook for 30 minutes. Stir in the chicken livers. ☐ ☐ Make balls or croquettes of risotto using your hands, putting a little mozzarella and sauce in the middle of each one. Then dip each croquette in breadcrumbs. Heat the oil or lard in a deep pan and briskly deep-fry the croquettes a few at a time. Remove when golden brown and drain on paper towels. Keep hot until all the croquettes are cooked. Serve hot. ☐ ☐ When you cut the croquettes to eat them, the melted cheese inside forms long strands. The imaginative Romans call this dish 'telephone cords'!

SARDINES WITH PEPPER AND TOMATO SAUCE
For recipe, see p.65

COOKED HAM IN GELATIN
For recipe, see p.68

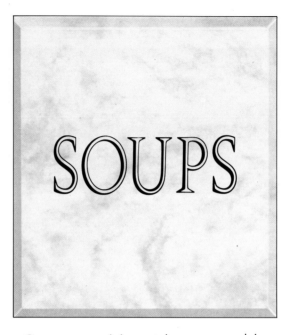

SOUPS

Soup would not be served in Italy at the same meal as pasta, because it often contains pasta itself. An Italian soup may be a delicate consommé garnished with dumplings or eggs, or it may be a nourishing broth thickened with rice and vegetables. Offer parmesan cheese with anything other than a fish soup.

PASSATO DI POMODORO ALLA PANNA
Creamed tomato soup

Ingredients/serves 4	I small carton thick cream
2kg/4 lb ripe tomatoes	Juice of ½ lemon
I teaspoon sugar	100g/4 oz chopped cooked ham
½ onion	½ cucumber, diced
Salt .	I teaspoon chopped basil
I teaspoon Worcestershire sauce	

LAZIO, UMBRIA AND THE MARCHES

Blanch and peel the tomatoes. De-seed and cut them into slices, then press through a strainer or blend to a purée. Pour into a pan, add the sugar and chill. Slice the onion, put it in a cloth and squeeze the juice into the tomato purée. Season with salt, add Worcestershire sauce, cream and lemon juice. Stir in the ham and cucumber, sprinkle with basil and serve.

ZUPPA DI CECI ALLA CONTADINA
Country chickpea soup

Ingredients/serves 4	2 tablespoons oil
500g/I lb chickpeas	150g/5 oz skinned and chopped tomatoes
50g/2 oz chopped pancetta	
I spring onion, chopped	Salt and pepper
I clove of garlic, sliced	200g/7 oz chopped lean pork
I tablespoon chopped parsley	4 slices of toast
A pinch of marjoram	100g/4 oz grated parmesan cheese

ABRUZZI-MOLISE

Soak the chickpeas in tepid water for 12 hours. Put the pancetta, spring onion, garlic, parsley and marjoram into a pan. Stir in the oil, chickpeas and tomatoes and add water. Salt and bring to the boil. Add the pork, cover and cook over a moderate heat for 2 hours. Season with a pinch of pepper and mix. Lay slices of the toast in the bottom of 4 soup bowls and pour the soup on. Pass the parmesan separately.

ZUPPA DI FAGIOLI ALLA MARCHIGIANA

BEAN AND VEGETABLE SOUP
For recipe, see p.76

MINESTRA AL PESTO

VEGETABLE SOUP WITH PESTO
For recipe, see p.76

MINESTRA AL PESTO
Vegetable soup with pesto

LIGURIA

Ingredients/serves 4	½ onion, sliced
250g/8oz spinach	2 tablespoons oil
200g/7oz green beans	Salt and pepper
2 potatoes, peeled and sliced	I tablespoon pesto sauce
½ white cabbage, chopped	200g/14oz rice
I leek, sliced	

Wash, trim and chop the spinach. Put it in a pan with the beans, potatoes, cabbage, leek and onion. Stir in oil to coat. Season and add 1.5lt/2pt water. Bring to the boil and cook over a medium heat for I hour. Stir in the pesto, pour on the rice and cook for a further 15 minutes. Serve at once. *Photograph page 74*

ZUPPA DI FAGIOLI ALLA MARCHIGIANA
Bean and vegetable soup

LAZIO, UMBRIA AND THE MARCHES

Ingredients/serves 4	I tablespoon tomato paste
150g/5oz chopped bacon	200g/7oz white cabbage
300g/10oz dried white beans, soaked	200g/7oz peeled and chopped potatoes
Salt and pepper	200g/7oz cauliflower florets
½ onion	I bunch of beets, cooked, peeled and diced
½ stalk of celery	
Parsley	4 slices of toast or bread baked hard
Oil	

Blanch the bacon, drain and put in a pan with the beans. Pour on 2lt/3½pt water, season with salt, and cook until the beans are done. Drain the beans and reserve the cooking liquor. □ □ Meanwhile, chop together the onion, celery and parsley and fry in a large pan in a little oil until soft. Add the tomato paste diluted with a little water. Pour over the bean cooking liquor and stir in the cabbage, potatoes, cauliflower and beets. Season. Simmer the soup for 30 minutes, adding more water if necessary. □ □ Meanwhile, purée half the beans and cook the peas separately. Add the bacon, beans and peas to the soup and heat through. Put the bread in a soup tureen and pour on the soup. Let it stand for a few minutes before serving. *Photograph page 74*

MINESTRONE ALLA MILANESE
Minestrone

LOMBARDY

Ingredients/serves 4	
1 strip belly pork	1 stalk of celery, finely chopped
500g/1lb fresh unshelled peas	350g/12oz skinned, deseeded and chopped ripe tomatoes
500g/1lb fresh unshelled borlotti beans	2 small firm courgettes, finely chopped
1 small bunch parsley	4 slices pancetta bacon, cut into strips
1 small bunch basil	2-3 potatoes, peeled and sliced
2 fresh sage leaves	100g/4oz rice
1 onion	1/4 savoy cabbage, shredded
1 clove of garlic	Salt and pepper
2 rashers fat bacon	5 tablespoons parmesan
50g/2oz butter	
1 carrot, finely chopped	

S crape the belly pork, put in a pan of cold water and boil for 5 minutes, then plunge into cold water and let it cool. Cut into strips. Pod the peas and beans and put them in separate bowls of cold water. Trim and chop the parsley, basil and sage together with the onion, garlic and fat bacon. Put the herb mixture in a large pan with half the butter, carrot, celery, tomatoes and courgettes. Add the pancetta and cook, stirring often, until the onion has softened and the bacon fat melted. Pour on 2lt/3⅓pt boiling water, salt lightly, and bring back to the boil. Add the drained beans and pork, stir and cook for 2 hours. □ □ Add the potatoes, rice, cabbage and peas, and cook, uncovered, until the rice is al dente, stirring often. Be careful not to overcook the rice, remembering it will continue to cook in the hot soup when removed from the heat. □ □ Season to taste, swirl in the remaining butter and 1 tablespoon parmesan. Allow to cool. Ladle into soup bowls and dust with parmesan. □ □ This soup is best served cool or cold, but not chilled.

RICE AND TURNIP SOUP
For recipe, see p.81

MALFATTINI ALLA ROMAGNOLA

CRAZY-CUT PASTA ROMAGNOLA STYLE
For recipe, see p.82

MINESTRONE DI VERDURA ALLA LIVORNESE

Minestrone Livorno style

TUSCANY

Ingredients/serves 4	
500g/1 lb toscanelli beans	100g/4 oz carrots, cut into julienne
2 tablespoons chopped parsley	1 stalk of celery, cut into julienne
1 slice prosciutto	1 courgette, cut into julienne
1 clove of garlic	1 stock cube
Olive oil	350g/12 oz skinned and deseeded ripe tomatoes
½ small savoy cabbage, shredded	100g/4 oz belly pork, trimmed and cut into strips
150g/5 oz trimmed, washed and shredded spinach *or* spinach beet leaves	Salt
1 onion, chopped	150g/5 oz rice
300g/10 oz peeled potatoes, cut into julienne	5 tablespoons parmesan cheese

P od the beans and put them into cold water. Trim, wash and finely chop the parsley, together with the prosciutto and garlic. Put them in a pan with 3 tablespoons oil. Cook for a few minutes, then add the cabbage and spinach, stir and cook over a moderate heat. Add the onion and julienne of potatoes, carrots, celery and courgette. □ □ Pour on 1.5lt/2 pt water, add the stock cube, tomatoes and belly pork. When the water comes to the boil, add the drained beans, cover and simmer gently for 2 hours. Season to taste, add the rice, stir and cook, uncovered until the rice is done. The soup should be thick. Remove from the heat and stir in 2 tablespoons parmesan. Serve the rest separately.

STRACCIATELLA ALLA ROMANA

Egg noodle soup

LAZIO, UMBRIA AND THE MARCHES

Ingredients/serves 4	
3 eggs	50g/2 oz grated parmesan
3 tablespoons fine semolina	1.7lt/3 pt meat stock
1 tablespoon chopped parsley	Salt
	Nutmeg

I n a bowl, beat the eggs with the semolina and parsley and half the parmesan. Pour on a cup of cold stock, season with salt and nutmeg and whisk. Bring the remaining stock to the boil, pour in the semolina mixture and stir for 3-4 minutes over a moderate heat until fine shreds of egg form. Serve at once and pass the remaining cheese round.

MINESTRA DI RISO E RAPE ALLA MILANESE
Rice and turnip soup

Ingredients/serves 4	2 medium turnips, peeled
25g/1 oz parsley	and thinly sliced
2 bacon rashers *or*	1.25lt/2¼pt meat stock
pancetta bacon	200g/7 oz rice
butter	6 tablespoons parmesan

LOMBARDY

Wash and chop the parsely together with the bacon. Fry for a few minutes in a little butter. Then add the turnip and cook for a few more minutes. Add the stock, bring to the boil and simmer for 7 minutes. Add the rice, stir and cook uncovered until just al dente. A minute before removing from the heat, stir in 2 tablespoons parmesan, then serve with the remaining cheese separately. ☐ ☐ If the turnips are very young and tender you can add them when you put in the rice.

Photograph page 78

MINESTRA DI PASTA ALL'UOVO E PISELLI
Egg pasta and pea soup

Ingredients/serves 4	1 tablespoon tomato paste
½ carrot, chopped	Salt and pepper
½ onion, chopped	200g/7 oz shelled young peas
½ stalk of celery, chopped	(petits pois)
1 tablespoon chopped parsley	200g/7 oz small egg pasta shapes
25g/1 oz butter	100g/4 oz grated parmesan

VENETO

Gently fry the chopped vegetables and parsley in a pan with the butter until golden brown. Add the tomato paste diluted with 2 tablespoons water, season and cook for 10 minutes. Pour on 1.5lt/ 2½ pt water, bring to the boil and add the peas. Cook for 25 minutes, add the pasta and cook for a further 25 minutes. Serve at once, handing the grated cheese separately.

MALFATTINI ALLA ROMAGNOLA
Crazy-cut pasta Romagnola style

EMILIA-
ROMAGNA

Ingredients/serves 4	Salt
300g/10 oz flour	A pinch of nutmeg
3 eggs, beaten	

Heap the flour on the work surface, make a well in the middle and add the eggs and a pinch of salt and nutmeg. Form into a dough and knead the mixture until it is smooth. □ □ Form the dough into a rectangular loaf shape and leave to dry out a little. Cut it into thick slices and let it dry a little longer. Chop coarsely and dry out completely. Pour the stock into a pan and bring to the boil. Add the pasta and cook for 2-3 minutes, then serve in soup bowls. *Photograph page 79*

TIELLA ALLA PUGLIESE
Mussel and potato soup

APULIA

Ingredients/serves 4	½ small onion
750g/1½ lb mussels	1 clove of garlic
Oil	300g/10 oz peeled and sliced
Salt and freshly ground black	potatoes
pepper	200g/7 oz rice
2 rashers fat bacon	

Scrape the mussels and rinse them well under cold running water. Cook in a large pan over a gentle heat with a little oil and a pinch of freshly ground pepper until they open. Drain them, discarding any that remain closed, and reserve the strained liquid. Remove the mussels from their shells. □ □ Chop the bacon, onion and garlic finely together and put into a pan with 1 tablespoon oil. Pour on 1.25lt/2¼ pt water, add the potatoes, season with salt and bring to the boil. Simmer for 10 minutes, then add the rice and cook briskly. □ □ Just before the soup is cooked, strain the mussel cooking liquor and add to the soup with the mussels. Heat through for a couple of minutes and serve. *Photograph page 85*

CACCIUCCO
Tuscan fish soup

Ingredients/serves 4	Olive oil
1kg/2 lb assorted fresh fish, large and small	1 large onion, thinly sliced
	1 stalk of celery, thinly sliced
600g/1 ¼ lb assorted seafood including squid, octopus, prawns etc	1 carrot, thinly sliced
	Salt and pepper
	1 glass dry white wine
400g/14 oz mussels *or* clams	3 medium ripe tomatoes,
4 tablespoons chopped parsley	peeled, deseeded and sliced
3 cloves of garlic	4 large *or* 8 small slices
1 red chilli pepper	firm white bread

TUSCANY

This delicious fish soup can easily be a main course in itself. Any fish can be used: mullet, eel, Moray eel, scampi, crayfish etc, provided it is very fresh. □ □ Clean the fish, keeping the heads to one side, leaving the small fish whole and cutting the big ones into regular sized chunks. Wash and drain well. Clean and prepare the squid and octopus. Then clean and scrape the mussels and clams, washing very well. Soaking for a couple of hours helps to get rid of any sand. □ □ Wash and trim the parsley and chop it together with 2 cloves of garlic and the chilli pepper. Put this mixture with ½ glass oil into a large earthenware dish over a moderate heat. Add the onion, celery and carrot, season and fry gently, stirring well. Then add the seafood and fish and cook gently, gradually adding the wine and stirring. When the wine has evaporated add the mussels or clams. When they have opened, remove and reserve. Add the tomatoes and continue cooking until the squid is done, adding a little water, if necessary. □ □ Meanwhile, poach the fish heads separately in water for about 15-20 minutes. Bone them, and push the flesh through the strainer or purée in a blender. Stir the purée into the soup. If the mixture is very thick, add a little boiling water and season to taste □ □ Preheat the oven to 190°C (/375°F/Gas 5. Rub the bread with the remaining clove of garlic and put on a baking sheet in the oven. When the bread has hardened, lay slices in a large tureen or in individual soup bowls. When the soup is done, remove the bones if you wish, check the seasoning and pour over the bread. Serve immediately, accompanied by the same wine used for cooking.

Photograph page 84

CACCIUCCO

TUSCAN FISH SOUP
For recipe, see p.83

TIELLA ALLA PUGLIESE

MUSSEL AND POTATO SOUP
For recipe, see p.83

PASTA

Pasta is traditionally made at home in the centre and north of Italy, and produced in factories and sold in packets in the south. Now, with more women out at work, both fresh and dried pasta are readily available in the shops, but there is still nothing quite like making it yourself.

SPAGHETTI AGLIO E OLIO
Spaghetti with garlic and oil

Ingredients/serves 4	3 cloves of garlic
500g/1 lb spaghetti	1 hot red chilli
Salt and pepper	5 tablespoons chopped parsley
1 glass virgin olive oil	

CAMPANIA

For this Neapolitan dish you should use the very best olive oil. Put plenty of salted water on to boil and cook the pasta until al dente. Halfway through pasta cooking time, heat the oil in a pan and add the garlic cloves and chilli. Fry until the garlic has turned dark, then remove the garlic and chilli. Drain the pasta. Pour into a bowl. Add the parsley to the oil, pour it into the bowl onto the spaghetti, add freshly ground pepper and serve immediately.

SPAGHETTI ALLA PUTTANESCA
Spaghetti with hot sauce

Ingredients/serves 4	½ glass olive oil
Salt	2 cloves of garlic, crushed
150g/5oz ripe olives	1 red chilli , chopped
4 or 5 anchovies in brine	1 tablespoon tomato paste
500g/1 lb ripe tomatoes	359g/12 oz spaghetti
1 tablespoon capers in brine	

CAMPANIA

Put on a pan of salted water to boil for the pasta. Pit the olives, wash and fillet the anchovies. Blanch, skin and deseed the tomatoes. Wash the capers thoroughly to get rid of excess saltiness. □ □ Put the oil into a pan with the garlic, chilli and anchovies and fry, stirring. Add the tomatoes, tomato paste, capers and olives and cook briskly for a few minutes, stirring often. □ □ Cook the spaghetti in boiling water until al dente, drain, stir in the sauce and serve. *Photograph page 89*

SPAGHETTI CON LE VONGOLE

SPAGHETTI WITH CLAMS
For recipe, see p.90

SPAGHETTI ALLA PUTTANESCA

SPAGHETTI WITH HOT SAUCE
For recipe, see p.87

SPAGHETTI CON LE VONGOLE
Spaghetti with clams

CAMPANIA

Ingredients/serves 4	2 cloves of garlic, crushed
1.3kg/2½lb clams	½ glass olive oil
Salt and pepper	500g/1 lb spaghetti *or* trenette
750g/1½ lb ripe tomatoes	2 tablespoons chopped parsley

Wash the clams thoroughly, rinsing away any sand. If possible, leave to soak in cold salted water for 1-2 hours. Put them in a large pan, cover and cook over a gentle heat, shaking occasionally until all the clams are open. □ □ Remove the clams from their shells and transfer to a bowl. If they still have sand in them when cooked, rinse in tepid water. Strain the clam cooking liquor through a cloth and add it to the clams. □ □ Blanch, skin, de-seed and chop the tomatoes, or press through a strainer, if you prefer. Fry the crushed garlic in oil until lightly browned. Add the tomatoes, clam liquor and a pinch of pepper and cook over a high heat, stirring often. □ □ Cook the spaghetti in plenty of boiling salted water until al dente. A minute before draining the pasta, add the clams and parsley to the tomatoes, bring to the boil and remove from the heat immediately. □ □ Drain the pasta, transfer to a serving dish, mix in the sauce and serve. *Photograph page 89*

SPAGHETTI ALLA CARBONARA
Spaghetti with bacon and eggs

LAZIO, UMBRIA
AND
THE MARCHES

Ingredients/serves 4-5	4 tablespoons double cream
100g/4 oz pancetta bacon, diced	Salt and pepper
40g/1½ oz butter	500g/1 lb spaghetti
4 eggs	50g/2 oz grated parmesan cheese

Fry the pancetta in butter, remove with a slotted spoon and keep hot. Beat the eggs in a bowl with a pinch of pepper and the cream. Cook the spaghetti until al dente in plenty of boiling salted water, drain, pour into a bowl with the eggs and mix well. Sprinkle with the pancetta and parmesan and serve at once.

VERMICELLI PICCANTI ALLA CALABRESE
Spicy vermicelli

Ingredients/serves 4	4 small anchovies
500g/1 lb vermicelli	1 clove of garlic
Salt	Oil
2 hot chillies, chopped	1 tablespoon chopped parsley

CALABRIA

Boil the vermicelli in plenty of salted water until al dente, drain and put on a serving dish. ☐ ☐ Meanwhile prepare the sauce. De-salt the anchovies and pound in a mortar. Fry the garlic in oil until soft. Add the chillies, anchovies and parsley. Pour the sauce on the vermicelli and serve.

RAVIOLI ALLA SALVIA CON LA ZUCCA
Ravioli with sage and pumpkin

Ingredients/serves 4	Whole grain mustard, or Italian
For the pasta	fruity mustard, if available
400g/14 oz flour	Salt and pepper
Salt	A pinch of nutmeg
5 eggs	*For the sauce*
1 teaspoon oil	100g/4 oz melted and browned
For the filling	butter
2kg/4¼ lb pumpkin	A few leaves of sage
100g/4 oz grated parmesan cheese	50g/2 oz grated parmesan cheese
4 amaretti biscuits, crushed	Salt

LIGURIA

Preheat the oven to 200°C/400°F/Gas 6. Make the pasta according to the instructions on pp.51-52. For the filling, cook the pumpkin whole in the oven and scrape the flesh into a bowl. Stir in the parmesan, amaretti crumbs, and mustard. Season with salt, pepper and a pinch of nutmeg and mix well. Make the ravioli according to the instructions onp.55, placing the filling at 5cm/2 inch intervals. Boil the ravioli in plenty of salted water until al dente. Drain and arrange in layers with the melted butter, sage and parmesan, finishing with a sprinkling of parmesan. Bake in the oven until golden brown. *Photograph page 92*

RAVIOLI ALLA SALVIA CON LA ZUCCA

*R*AVIOLI WITH SAGE AND PUMPKIN
For recipe, see p.91

*B*OLOGNESE TORTELLINI PIE
For recipe, see p.96

RAVIOLI CON LA RICOTTA

Ravioli with ricotta

LAZIO, UMBRIA
AND
THE MARCHES

Ingredients/serves 4	50g/2oz grated parmesan cheese
For the pasta	
400g/14oz flour	1 egg, plus 1 yolk
1 tablespoon oil	Salt and pepper
4 eggs and a little water, or 5 eggs	To serve
	2-4 tablespoons melted butter, browned
Salt	
For the filling	Sage leaves, chopped
500g/1 lb ricotta cheese	Grated parmesan

P our the flour into a mound on the work surface. Make a well in the top and add the oil, eggs and a pinch of salt. Work the ingredients in together, adding a little water if you are using 4 eggs, to make dough. Knead until pliable. Allow the dough to rest for 30 minutes. ☐ ☐ Combine the ingredients for the filling. ☐ ☐ Roll out the dough and prepare the ravioli as on pp.51 and 55. Boil in plenty of salted water until al dente. Transfer to a hot serving dish and pour over the melted butter. Sprinkle over some fresh sage and plenty of parmesan to serve. ☐ ☐ The ravioli can also be served with a tomato sauce flavoured with a little basil.

MACCHERONCINI CON I GAMBERI

Macaroni with prawns

VENETO

Ingredients/serves 4	500g/1 lb macaroni
1 teaspoon thyme	2 cloves of garlic, crushed
1 bay leaf	Oil
2 tablespoons chopped parsley	1 red chilli
Salt	400g/14oz peeled and chopped tomatoes
400g/14oz prawns	

P ut the thyme, bay leaf, half the parsley and a pinch of salt into a pan of water, bring to the boil and add the prawns. Cook for 3 minutes, then drain. Peel and roughly chop the prawns. ☐ ☐ Cook the macaroni in plenty of boiling salted water until al dente. Fry the garlic in the oil, add the chilli and tomatoes, season with salt and cook for 10 minutes. Add the prawns. Drain the pasta, mix in the sauce and sprinkle on the remaining chopped parsley.

Ravioli alla Panna Gratinati
Gratin of ravioli with cream

Ingredients/serves 4	25g/1oz breadcrumbs
For the pasta	2 egg yolks
400g/14oz flour	Salt and pepper
5 eggs	2 tablespoons grated parmesan
1 tablespoon oil	cheese
Salt	*For the sauce*
For the filling	75g/3oz butter
50g/2oz onion, chopped	5 tablespoons grated parmesan
40g/1½oz butter	cheese
100g/4oz finely-diced sausage	Small carton single cream

EMILIA-ROMAGNA

P reheat the oven to 200°C/400°F/Gas 6. Make the pasta according to the instructions on pp.51-52. For the filling, soften the onion in the butter, add the sausage, breadcrumbs and seasoning and cook gently for 10 minutes. Transfer the sauce to a bowl and allow it to cool. Mix in the yolks and parmesan. ☐ ☐ Assemble the ravioli according to the instructions on p.55. ☐ ☐ Boil the ravioli in plenty of salted water for about 7 minutes, or until they rise to the top and have lost their pasty appearance. Drain and arrange in a baking dish in layers with knobs of butter, the cheese and cream. Bake in the oven until golden brown.

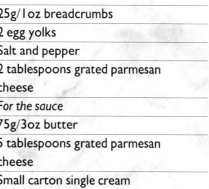

Bucatini all'Amatriciana
Bucatini with bacon and tomatoes

Ingredients/serves 4	Salt and white pepper
100g/4oz guanciale bacon, chopped	500g/1 lb bucatini (or other pasta shapes)
25g/1oz lard	50g/2oz grated pecorino
1 small onion, finely chopped	cheese
400g/14oz skinned, deseeded and chopped firm ripe tomatoes	

LAZIO, UMBRIA AND THE MARCHES

P ut on plenty of salted water to boil for the pasta. Put the bacon in a saucepan with the lard and onion and fry until the bacon has browned. Add the tomatoes, season a little and cook briskly for about 10 minutes. Meanwhile, cook the pasta until al dente, drain and transfer to the bowl. Add the cheese and sauce, stir and serve hot.

PASTICCIO DI TORTELLINI ALLA BOLOGNESE
Bolognese tortellini pie

EMILIA-ROMAGNA

Ingredients/serves 4	200g/7oz loin of pork, finely chopped
For the pasta	200g/7oz lean minced beef
400g/14oz flour	100g/4oz prosciutto, finely chopped
4 eggs	
For the filling	100g/4oz butter
50g/2oz butter	2 tablespoons tomato sauce
300g/10oz lanza sausage, chopped	1 clove
	1 bay leaf
100g/4oz mortadella, chopped	Salt and pepper
150g/5oz turkey fillet, chopped	Small carton double cream
100g/4oz prosciutto, chopped	4-5 chicken livers
1 egg	*For the pastry*
100g/4oz grated parmesan cheese	300g/10oz flour
	Salt
Nutmeg	150g/5oz butter, softened and cut into small pieces
Salt and pepper	
For the sauce	Egg yolk (optional)
1 carrot	1-2 tablespoons white wine
1 onion	A little grated lemon peel (optional)
1 stick of celery	
100g/4oz pancetta bacon	

It is recommended that you prepare the filling for the pasta and the sauce 1 or 2 days ahead of time and the pastry on the next day, as there is a fair amount of work involved. Put the pasticcio together on the day you want to serve it. ☐ ☐ For the filling, melt the butter in a pan. Add the sausages, turkey and prosciutto and cook gently, stirring. Remove from the heat. Stir in the egg, half the parmesan and the seasoning and use to fill the tortellini. ☐ ☐ For the sauce, prepare and then chop together carrot, onion, celery and bacon and put in a pan with the pork, beef and ham and fry gently with half the butter, stirring until the vegetables have softened and meat has changed colour. Add the tomato sauce diluted in a glass of water, the clove and bay leaf. Season, stir and cook very gently for an hour, adding the cream when it starts to dry out. 5 minutes before the end of cooking time, wash the chicken livers thoroughly and chop them. Add to the sauce.

☐ ☐ Prepare the pasta according to the instructions given in the Basic Recipe Section, p.51-52. Let it rest, then make the tortellini, as on page 54-55.

☐ ☐ For the pastry, pour the flour onto a board, make a well in the centre and put in a pinch of salt, the butter, egg yolk and white wine (plus a little grated lemon peel, if liked). Mix together with the fingertips, but do not work longer than necessary. Roll into a ball, wrap and chill for an hour, or overnight if preferred. ☐ ☐ To assemble the pasticcio, put a pan of salted water on to boil and cook the tortellini, removing them while still very al dente. Transfer them to a bowl, add the sauce, the rest of the butter, less 1 tablespoon, and the remaining parmesan and mix well. Allow to cool. ☐ ☐ Grease a deep cake tine or pie dish, dust with breadcrumbs, and shake out the excess. Preheat the oven to 180°C/350°/Gas 4. ☐ ☐ Remove the pastry from the fridge and cut into two pieces, one twice as big as the other. Roll out the bigger piece into a circle large enough to line the cake tin and put it in. Put a layer of tortellini in the bottom, cover with sauce, another layer of tortellini and so on until they are all used up. Roll out a circle of pastry to cover the pasticcio, press it on at the edges, dampening them first, and decorate with pastry trimmings (diamonds, hearts, half-moons etc). Prick with a fork and bake for about 40 minutes. Let the pasticcio stand for 10 minutes. *Photograph page 93*

RICCHIE I PRIVIETI ALLA CALABRESE
Ricchie with meat and pecorino sauce

Ingredients/serves 4	For the sauce
For the pasta	250g/8oz meat and tomato
400g/14oz flour	sauce (see p.47)
4 eggs	100g/4oz grated pecorino cheese
1 teaspoon oil	Salt
1 pinch of salt	
or 400g/14 oz ricchie (pasta shaped like little ears)	

CALABRIA

E ither buy ready-made ricchie, or make fresh pasta with the ingredients given (see pp.51-52). Let the dough rest for 30 minutes, then cut it into little discs. With a floured thumb, press each disc into the shape of an ear. Allow to dry. ☐ ☐ .Boil the ricchie in plenty of salted water until al dente. Drain and mix in the meat sauce and 2 tablespoons pecorino. Serve the remaining cheese separately. *Photograph page 101*

Zite Ripieni Stufate alla Casertana

Stuffed braised zite

CAMPANIA

Ingredients/serves 4	Nutmeg
1 teaspoon chopped onion	2 eggs, beaten
75g/3oz pork kidney fat	500g/1 lb zite (big macaroni)
400g/14oz minced pork	1 tablespoon breadcrumbs
100g/4oz salami, derinded and minced	400ml/^{2}/$_3$ pint tomato sauce
Salt and pepper	75g/3oz grated caciocavallo cheese

Preheat the oven to 200°C/400°F/Gas 6. Fry the onion in half the kidney fat, add the pork and salami. Season, add a pinch of nutmeg and cook for 20 minutes. Remove the sauce from the heat, allow it to cool and stir in the eggs. Boil the zite in plenty of salted water until al dente. Drain and allow to cool, then fill with the stuffing. ☐ ☐ Grease a casserole dish with the remaining kidney fat and sprinkle with breadcrumbs. Arrange the stuffed zite in layers with the tomato sauce and the cheese. Put the dish in the oven for 20-30 minutes until golden brown on top. Serve at once.

Photograph page 101

Cappelletti con Ripieno

Cappelletti with chicken stuffing

EMILIA-ROMAGNA

Ingredients/serves 4	150g/5oz grated mascarpone cheese
For the pasta	
250g/8oz flour	1 egg
2 eggs	7 tablespoons grated parmesan cheese
For the filling and sauce	
50g/2oz prosciutto, chopped	Salt and pepper
100g/4oz butter	1 teaspoon flour
250g/8oz cooked chicken breast	Scant teaspoon meat extract
Good quality cognac	Small carton double cream

For the filling, put the prosciutto in a small pan with 25g/1oz butter and fry for 1 minute. Add the chicken and cognac and cook on a low heat without letting the meat brown. ☐ ☐ Meanwhile, pour the flour onto a board and make a well in the centre. Break the eggs into it and mix together well. Put the dough into a plastic bag and close it tightly.

□ □ When the chicken is cooked, remove it from the pan and chop very finely. Put it into a bowl, add the cooking juices, mascarpone, egg and half the parmesan. Season and stir well. □ □ Roll out the pasta and make cappelletti (see pp. 51-52 and 54). Stuff them with the filling. Then put on a floured tray, not letting them touch. Put salted water on to boil. □ □ Blend the flour and meat extract into the cream without letting lumps form. Put the remaining butter on to melt, then add the cream mixture. Let it boil, stirring, for 2 minutes, then set aside and keep warm. □ □ Boil the cappelletti in salted water and remove with a slotted spoon. Put a layer of pasta into a dish, pour on some cream sauce, sprinkle with parmesan, add another layer of cappelletti, a layer of sauce and so on until all the ingredients have been used up. □ □ Serve hot.

TORTELLONI CON PASTA VERDE AL GRATIN
Spinach tortelloni bake

LAZIO, UMBRIA
AND
THE MARCHES

Ingredients/serves 4	
For the pasta	I egg yolk
400g/14oz flour	Nutmeg
250g/8oz fresh spinach,	Salt and pepper
cooked, puréed and thoroughly	*For the sauce*
drained	I small onion, chopped
4 eggs	2 tablespoons olive oil
For the filling	100g/4oz sieved tomatoes
250g/8oz ricotta cheese	Basil leaves, chopped
500g/1lb fresh spinach, cooked,	Salt and pepper
puréed and thoroughly drained	50g/2oz butter
75g/3oz cooked prosciutto,	3 tablespoons grated parmesan
chopped	cheese
3 tablespoons grated parmesan	I mozzarella cheese, sliced
cheese	

Prepare the pasta according to the instructions on pp.51-52. Make the filling by thoroughly mixing all the ingredients together. Cut out the pasta, fill and shape into tortelloni (see illustrations 1 and 2 on p.56). To make the sauce, soften the onion in the olive oil, stir in the tomato and basil leaves and season with salt and pepper. Cook the tortelloni until al dente. □ □ Layer the tortelloni in a buttered ovenproof dish with the butter, parmesan cheese and tomato sauce. Finish with a layer of mozzarella cheese and put into a hot oven (200°C/400°F/Gas 6) until the cheese melts. Serve hot. *Photograph page 56*

Ricchie with meat and pecorino sauce
For recipe, see p.97

Stuffed braised zite
For recipe, see p.98

PRIMI PIATTI

The 'first course' in Italy might be soup, rice or pasta, or it might be any of the following dishes, notably gnocchi or polenta — simple, sustaining foods that cost very little. Made with care and imagination, these dishes form the basis of a characteristic Italian meal.

PAPPA COL POMODORO
Thick tomato soup

Ingredients/serves 4	
800g/1¾ lb ripe tomatoes	250g/8oz slightly stale bread (about 2 days old), cubed
4 tablespoons virgin olive oil	Salt and black pepper
3 cloves garlic, crushed	1lt/2pt meat stock
A few leaves of sage and basil	

TUSCANY

Wash and skin the tomatoes. Remove the seeds from half, push the other half through a strainer. Heat the oil in a pan and add the crushed garlic, sage and basil. Cook for 1-2 minutes, then add the bread and fry all over until golden brown. Add all the tomatoes, season and cook for 10 minutes, stirring. Gradually add the stock and cook until you have a thick, soupy consistency. It can be served hot, cold or warm, but do not refrigerate.

SPIEDINI DI FONTINA
Fontina kebabs

Ingredients/serves 4	
300g/10 oz fontina cheese	300ml/½ pt hot béchamel sauce
100g/4oz smoked pancetta bacon	Salt and pepper
	100g/4oz flour
8 square slices of bread	200g/7oz breadcrumbs
1 egg and 2 yolks	Oil

LAZIO, UMBRIA
AND
THE MARCHES

Cut the fontina and pancetta into 20 cubes each. Remove the crusts from the bread and divide each slice into quarters. Onto 4 skewers put 5 cubes of cheese, alternating with slices of bread and 5 pieces of pancetta. Add 2 yolks to the hot béchamel with a pinch of pepper and dip the skewers into it to coat. Allow to cool, then dip in the flour. ☐ ☐ Beat the remaining egg with a pinch of salt and dip the kebabs in that and finally into the breadcrumbs. Fry in hot oil until golden brown. Drain on kitchen paper, put on a dish and serve.

TORTA PASQUALINA

SORREL AND EGG PIE
For recipe, see p.107

PUCCIA ALLA PIEMONTESE

POLENTA WITH PORK AND CABBAGE
For recipe, see p.106

PUCCIA ALLA PIEMONTESE
Polenta with pork and cabbage

PIEDMONT

Ingredients/serves 4	1 onion
300g/10 oz corn meal	1 carrot
25g/1 oz flour	1 stalk of celery
1.5lt/2 pt water	Salt and pepper
Salt	150g/5 oz butter, diced
1 curly cabbage	100g/4 oz grated
750g/1½ lb lean pork (leg if possible)	parmesan cheese

Prepare the polenta with corn meal, flour, water and salt according to the instructions on p.59. Remove tough outer leaves and stalks from the cabbage, cut into quarters, and boil in salted water. Drain and set aside. □ □ Put the pork in a flameproof casserole, cover with cold water, bring to the boil and add the onion, carrot and celery. Season and simmer until just cooked. Transfer the meat to a plate and cut into cubes. □ □ Pass the stock through a fine strainer. Pour a cupful back into the casserole and add the meat and cabbage. Add the prepared polenta and mix well. Remove from the heat, stir in the butter and parmesan and mix well. Serve in soup plates. *Photograph page 105*

POLENTA TARAGNA
Buckwheat polenta

VENETO

Ingredients/serves 4	150g/5 oz finely ground corn meal
200g/7 oz buckwheat flour	100g/4 oz butter, diced
Salt	100g/4 oz soft white cheese, sliced

Pour the buckwheat flour into a large saucepan and gradually add 1.25lt/2 pt cold water, stirring continuously to prevent lumps forming. Add a pinch of salt, put the polenta onto a moderate heat and bring to the boil, stirring all the time. When it begins to boil, add the corn meal. Continue to cook, stirring, for 30 minutes. Add the butter and cook for a further 20 minutes, still stirring. Then add the cheese, cook until melted and pour the polenta onto a serving plate. The cheese should be well mixed in so that you can see strands of white cheese against the darker polenta. *Photograph page 108*

TORTA PASQUALINA
Sorrel and egg pie

Ingredients/serves 4	100g/4 oz grated
600g/1 ¼ lb flour	parmesan cheese
Oil	Marjoram
Salt and pepper	9 eggs
1kg/2 lb sorrel	400g/14 oz ricotta cheese

LIGURIA

Pour the flour onto a board and make a well, then mix in 2 tablespoons oil, a pinch of salt and enough tepid water to give a smooth pliable dough. Knead for 10 minutes. Divide into 14 pieces and shape each one into a ball. Dust with flour, put under a cloth and leave to stand for an hour. Preheat the oven 200°C/400°F/Gas 6. □ □ Wash the sorrel, discarding any discoloured leaves and large stalks. Put it in a pan with only the water clinging to it, cover and cook gently over a low heat, stirring occasionally to make sure it does not stick to the pan. When it is cooked (about 8 minutes), squeeze the water out of it, chop and add half the grated parmesan, a pinch of marjoram, 3 eggs and the ricotta. Season and knead the mixture. □ □ Roll out one of the pastry balls very thinly and lay on a greased baking sheet. Sprinkle it with a few drops of oil. Roll out the second pastry ball and lay it on top of the first. Continue oiling the pastry layers until you have 7 layers. Put the sorrel filling on top. Make 6 dents in the sorrel mixture with back of a spoon and into each break an egg. Season and sprinkle with the remaining cheese. Roll out the other 7 balls until very thin and lay them on top, greasing with oil as before. Prick the top sheet with a fork, brush with a little oil and bake in the oven for an hour. Allow to cool and serve cold. *Photograph page 104*

FRITTATA DI SCALOGNI
Shallot omelette

Ingredients/serves 4	6 eggs
500g/1 lb shallots	Salt and pepper
A little flour	½ teaspoon thyme
3 tablespoons oil	

BASILICATA

Peel the shallots, boil until tender and drain. Dust lightly with flour and fry in oil. Beat the eggs in a bowl with a pinch of salt, pepper and the thyme. Add them to the shallots a in frying pan, stir with a wooden spoon and shake gently to prevent the mixture from sticking to the bottom. When it has started to set, invert the omelette, using a plate, and finish cooking. Serve very hot. *Photograph page 109*

POLENTA TARAGNA

BUCKWHEAT POLENTA
For recipe, see p.106

FRITTATA DI SCALOGNI

SHALLOT OMELET
For recipe, see p.107

GNOCCHI AL GORGONZOLA
Gnocchi with gorgonzola

VENETO

Ingredients/serves 4	For the sauce
For the gnocchi	50g/2 oz mild
600g/1¼ lb floury potatoes	gorgonzola cheese
300g/10 oz flour	100g/4 oz butter
1 egg	Pepper
Grappa	3 tablespoons grated
Salt	parmesan cheese
	4 tablespoons double cream, warmed

Prepare the gnocchi according to the instructions on pp. 57-58. Put a pan of salted water on to boil and warm a bowl. Remove the rind from the gorgonzola and cut the cheese into small pieces. Put in a bowl with the butter and a pinch of pepper and blend to a cream with a wooden spoon. Stir in the parmesan and heated cream. Keep warm. □ □ Put the gnocchi into the boiling water. Stir and cook briskly. When they come to the surface, remove with a slotted spoon and transfer to the bowl with the sauce. Stir well to coat with sauce and serve immediately.

GNOCCHI ALLA BAVA
Gnocchi with cheese

EMILIA-ROMAGNA

Ingredients/serves 4	For the sauce
For the gnocchi	150g/5oz butter, melted
600g/1¼ lb floury white potatoes	300g/10 oz fontina cheese, diced
250g/8 oz flour	6 tablespoons grated parmesan cheese
Salt	Salt

Prepare the gnocchi according to the instructions on pp.57-58 and bring a pan of salted water to the boil. Add the gnocchi carefully and cook over a high heat. As the gnocchi come to the surface, remove with a slotted ladle. Arrange them in layers in a hot bowl with melted butter, fontina and parmesan until all the ingredients are used up. □ □ Put the bowl over the pan of boiling gnocchi water (without letting any water in) for about 10 minutes until the cheese melts. Serve very hot.

Uova in Camicia con Peperoni
Poached eggs with red peppers

Ingredients/serves 4	1 tablespoon vinegar
4 red peppers	8 eggs
Oil	2 tablespoons grated
Salt	parmesan cheese
8 slices lean pancetta bacon	4 tablespoons melted butter

VENETO

Preheat the oven to 220°C/425°F/Gas 7. Bake the peppers until slightly charred. Turn the oven down to 200°C/400°F/Gas 6. Peel, slice and season the peppers with a little oil and salt. Blanch the pancetta and then fry for a few minutes with the peppers in a little oil. ☐ ☐ Bring a wide deep pan of salted water to the boil and add the vinegar. Break the eggs one by one into a saucer, slide them into the water and when the whites have set, drain and plunge into cold water. ☐ ☐ Grease a dish and arrange the pancetta slices on the bottom. Arrange the eggs and peppers on top and sprinkle with parmesan. Pour over melted butter, put into the oven for 5 minutes and serve.

Budino di Salmone
Salmon loaf

Ingredients/serves 4	4 medium potatoes
600g/1¼ lb salmon	25g/1 oz butter
1 small carrot	2 tablespoons chopped parsley
1 onion	3 eggs
1 stalk of celery	150ml/¼ pt milk
Salt and peppercorns	25g/1 oz flour

LAZIO, UMBRIA
AND
THE MARCHES

Preheat the oven to 180°C/350°F/Gas 4. ☐ ☐ Poach the salmon in a pan of water, with the carrot, onion, celery and a few peppercorns. Boil the potatoes without peeling in salted water until cooked. Peel and slice. Butter a casserole dish and put in alternating layers of potato and the salmon cut into strips. Sprinkle each layer with parsley and salt and pepper. Beat the eggs with the milk and flour and pour onto mixture. Cook in the oven for 30 minutes until the top is golden brown. Serve at once.

Pizza alla Napoletana
Neapolitan pizza

CAMPANIA

Ingredients/serves 4	1 batch pizza dough (see p. 60)
3 anchovies in brine	Oregano
3 medium firm ripe tomatoes	Coarse salt
1 mozzarella cheese	2 tablespoons olive oil

P reheat the oven to 245°C/475°F/Gas 9. Fillet and wash the anchovies and cut them into strips. Skin the tomatoes, remove the seeds and chop. Cube or slice the mozzarella and drain, if very wet. Roll out the pizza dough and lay on an oiled baking sheet. Arrange the anchovies, tomatoes and mozzarella on top. Sprinkle with oregano and salt, trickle over the olive oil and bake for 15 minutes.

Pizza Fantasia
Fancy pizza

CAMPANIA

Ingredients/serves 4	12 pitted green olives
1 batch pizza dough (see p. 60)	1 tablespoon capers
	4 small gherkins, sliced
400g/14oz peeled and chopped tomatoes	5 baby artichokes in oil, sliced
1 mozzarella cheese, cut into little cubes	Pepper
8 anchovy fillets in oil, drained and chopped	4 tablespoons olive oil

P reheat the oven to 245°C/475°F/Gas 9. Roll the dough out into a circle, put on an oiled baking sheet and cover with the tomatoes. Arrange the mozzarella, anchovies, olives, capers, gherkins and artichokes on top. Season with pepper and dribble over the oil. Cook in the oven for 45 minutes. *Photograph page 115*

PIZZA TOPPINGS

Topping for pizza marinara	**Topping for pizza 4 stagioni**	**Topping for pizza Margherita/Serves 4**
3 medium firm ripe tomatoes (not watery ones)	Cooked clams	Thin slivers of mozzarella cheese
2-3 cloves of garlic	Cooked mussels	Tomatoes
Oregano	Pitted ripe olives cut into pieces	Shredded basil
Olive oil	Strips of anchovies in brine	Grated pecorino cheese
Coarse salt	Marinated artichoke hearts	Salt
		Oil

Other suggested toppings:

Capers	Seafood (add near the end of cooking time)	Sliced sausage
Chopped, pitted black olives		Cubed fontina cheese
Chopped, pitted green olives	Flaked tuna	Gruyère, gorgonzola, gouda cheeses (grated or sliced)
Artichokes in oil	Cooked ham, cut into slices	
Mushrooms in oil	Cubed salami	Sliced hard-boiled eggs
Roast peppers cut into strips	Sliced pancetta bacon	Basil, marjoram, parsley

PIZZETTE CON LE ALICI

Individual pizzas with anchovies

Ingredients/serves 4	2 cloves of garlic, crushed
1 kg/2 lb fresh anchovies	2 tablespoons chopped parsley
1 batch pizza dough (see p. 60)	Olive oil
Salt and pepper	

CAMPANIA

P reheat the oven to 245°C/475°F/Gas 9. Remove the heads from the anchovies, wash and dry well. Use canned anchovies if fresh ones are not available. Roll the dough into 4 thin circles and put on a greased baking sheet. Arrange the anchovies on the pizzas and season with pepper and a little salt. Sprinkle with garlic and parsley and moisten with a few spoonfuls of oil. ☐ ☐ Cook in the oven for 30 minutes and serve at once.

Photograph page 115

*I*NDIVIDUAL PIZZAS WITH ANCHOVIES
For recipe, see p.113

*F*ANCY PIZZA
For recipe, see p.112

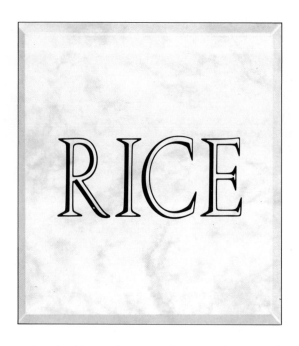

RICE

An Italian risotto is tender and moist, not dry, unlike the rice dishes of India and the Middle East. Serve it in soup plates, sprinkled with plenty of parmesan cheese.

RISOTTO ALLA SBIRRAGLIA
Chicken risotto

Ingredients/serves 4	
1 fresh chicken, cooked, giblets reserved	1 stalk of celery, chopped
	Salt and pepper
150g/5oz lean veal, chopped	1 glass dry white wine
1 carrot, chopped	3 medium tomatoes, chopped
1 onion, chopped	350g/12oz rice

LOMBARDY

Bone the chicken and dice the flesh. Put the veal, chicken bones and giblets into a pan with half the carrot, onion and celery. Cover with water, add a pinch of salt and cook the stock over a moderate heat. When it is ready (about 30 minutes), strain and keep hot. ☐ ☐ In a second pan, lightly brown the remaining vegetables in half the butter. Add the diced chicken, season and continue cooking, covered, for a few minutes. Pour on the wine, reduce by half, add the tomato and cook until soft. ☐ ☐ Pour on the rice and add a ladle of the stock. Continue adding the stock at intervals as the rice dries out. When it is cooked, remove the pan from the heat, stir in the remaining butter and half the parmesan. Serve with the remaining parmesan. *Photograph page 119*

RISOTTO ALL'USO DI SARDEGNA
Sardinian risotto with tomato sauce

Ingredients/serves 4	
75g/3oz butter	Oil
400g/14oz rice	1 clove of garlic
Salt and pepper	1/2 stick of celery
2 vegetable stock cubes	1/2 small onion
2 tablespoons grated pecorino	Small bunch of parsley
For the sauce	500g/1lb tomatoes, chopped
150g/5oz thick-cut lean pancetta bacon, chopped	Salt and pepper

SARDINIA

Heat half the butter in a pan, add the rice, season and cook for a few minutes. Pour on 1lt/2pt boiling water and crumble on the stock cubes. Stir as the rice absorbs the water. ☐ ☐ Meanwhile, fry the pancetta in a little oil, remove with a slotted spoon and set aside. Chop the vegetables and parsley together, add them to the cooking juices and lightly brown. Add the tomatoes, season and cook for 15 minutes. Finally, add the pancetta. Remove the rice from the heat, stir in the remaining butter and cheese and pour the hot sauce over. *Photograph page 118*

SARDINIAN RISOTTO WITH TOMATO SAUCE
For recipe, see p.117

CHICKEN RISOTTO
For recipe, see p.117

RISOTTO ALLA MILANESE

Milanese risotto

LOMBARDY

Ingredients/serves 4	I glass dry white wine
25g/I oz beef bone marrow	Ilt/2 pt meat stock, well
I small onion, thinly sliced	skimmed of fat
125g/5 oz butter	I sachet saffron
400g/14 oz rice	5 tablespoons parmesan cheese

S crape the marrow with a knife to remove any bits of bone, then chop and put in a pan with the onion and half the butter. Fry until the onion is soft but not brown. Add the rice and fry for 2 or 3 minutes. Add the wine and cook until absorbed. Add the stock with a ladle, waiting between each addition until it has been absorbed. Cook the rice for 30 minutes. 10 minutes before the end of the cooking time, dissolve the saffron in a few tablespoons of boiling stock and add to the rice. Finally, add the remaining butter and stir in the parmesan. Let it stand, covered, for 2 minutes before serving. *Photograph page 122*

RISOTTO ALLA PAESANA

Country-style risotto

LOMBARDY

Ingredients/serves 4	100g/4oz white beans, cooked
Oil	until al dente
I onion, chopped	Salt and pepper
100g/4 oz shelled peas	400g/14 oz rice
100g/4 oz asparagus tips	50g/2 oz butter
200g/7 oz courgettes, sliced	75g/3 oz grated parmesan
Stock	cheese
500g/I lb chopped tomatoes	

H eat a little oil in a pan and soften the onion. Add the peas, asparagus and courgettes and let the flavours mingle. Add a little stock and cook over a low heat for 10 minutes. Add the tomatoes and beans; season. Cook for 15 minutes, then add the rice. Stir and add more stock, as necessary, and cook until al dente. Stir in the butter and half the parmesan. Serve sprinkled with the remaining parmesan. *Photograph page 123*

RISOTTO ALLA TRASTEVERINA
Rice with ham and chicken livers

LAZIO, UMBRIA AND THE MARCHES

Ingredients/serves 4	100g/4 oz chicken livers, sliced
½ small onion, finely chopped	100g/4 oz prosciutto, cut into julienne
75g/3 oz butter, diced	
75g/3 oz lean pancetta bacon, diced	400g/14 oz rice
	Boiling stock
Salt and pepper	5 tablespoons grated parmesan cheese
1 glass dry marsala or red wine	

Fry the onion in half the butter, add the bacon, season and cook gently for 2 minutes. Add the marsala, or red wine, if preferred, and let it evaporate almost completely. Stir in the livers and ham. Add the rice and ladle on the stock gradually as the rice absorbs it, stirring constantly. Remove the risotto from the heat, stir in the remaining butter and a little parmesan. Leave to stand for 1 minute, then serve with the remaining parmesan. *Photograph page 127*

RISO CON CARCIOFI ALLA SICILIANA
Sicilian artichoke risotto

SICILY

Ingredients/serves 4	Oil
75g/3 oz fat bacon	100g/4 oz tomato flesh
1 onion	Salt and pepper
1 clove of garlic	300g/10 oz artichoke hearts
½ stalk of celery	200g/7 oz rice
A bunch of parsley	75g/3 oz grated pecorino cheese .

Chop together the bacon, onion, garlic, celery and parsley and fry in a few tablespoons of oil. Then add the tomato and crush with a fork. Season and cook gently for 10 minutes. □ □ Add the artichoke hearts and cold water and cook for a further 10 minutes. Bring to the boil, add the rice and cook for 20 minutes until just tender. Stir in the pecorino to serve.

RISOTTO ALLA MILANESE

MILANESE *RISOTTO*
For recipe, see p.120

RISOTTO ALLA PAESANA

COUNTRY-STYLE RISOTTO
For recipe, see p.120

RISOTTO CON LA ZUCCA

Pumpkin risotto

ABRUZZI-
MOLISE

Ingredients/serves 4	
500g/1 lb pumpkin	2 stock cubes
100g/4 oz butter	4 tablespoons grated parmesan cheese
400g/14 oz rice	Salt

C ut open the pumpkin and remove the seeds. Peel and cube the flesh. Put 1lt/2 pt water on to boil. Put the pumpkin and half the butter into a saucepan and fry for a minute, add a ladle of boiling water and cook gently until half cooked. ☐ ☐ Add the rice to the pumpkin, stir and fry for a minute, then add a ladle of boiling water and the stock cubes, stirring all the time and adding more water as each ladleful is absorbed. Continue the process until the rice is cooked. Turn off the heat, add the remaining butter and stir in the parmesan. Season with salt to taste and serve.

RISOTTO CON LE TINCHE ALLA LOMBARDA

Tench risotto

LOMBARDY

Ingredients/serves 4	
2 tench (250g/8 oz each)	75g/3 oz butter
1 onion	1 clove of garlic, chopped
1 carrot	1 small bunch of parsley, chopped
1 stalk of celery	400g/14 oz rice
Salt and pepper	

G ut, descale and wash the tench thoroughly in running water. Blanch them for a few minutes to get rid of the muddy taste. Then fillet them, reserving the bones etc. ☐ ☐ Make a fish stock with the discarded bits of fish, the onion, carrot and celery. Season, strain and keep warm. Melt half the butter in a pan, add the tench, season and cook gently. Keep warm. ☐ ☐ Melt the remaining butter in a separate pan and add the chopped parsley and garlic. When the garlic has softened, add the rice, stir for a few minutes and then gradually add the fish stock, ladle by ladle, until the rice has cooked. Stir to stop the rice sticking. Put the risotto into a deep dish, arrange the fish fillets on top and serve.

Photograph page 126

RISOTTO CON SCAMPI

Scampi risotto

Ingredients/serves 4	
75g/3 oz butter	A pinch of thyme
Oil	I glass dry white wine
½ carrot, chopped	500g/1lb fresh scampi, peeled
½ small onion, chopped	and cut into chunks
I stalk of celery, chopped	1.5lt/2½pt stock
I small glass brandy	400g/14 oz rice
	Salt

VENETO

Preheat the oven to 200°C/400°F/Gas 6. Heat half the butter with I tablespoon of oil in a pan and soften the chopped vegetables in it. Pour on the brandy and add the thyme. Cook gently, stirring, until the pan is dry. Then add the wine and reduce by half. Add the scampi and cook for 15 minutes. Keep the scampi sauce hot. ☐ ☐ Bring the stock to the boil, pour in the rice and add a pinch of salt. Bring back to the boil and then put in the oven for 20 minutes. Drain the rice, fluff it out with a fork, mix in the remaining butter and pour over the scampi sauce.

RISOTTO CON LE COZZE ALLA GONDOLIERA

Mussel risotto

Ingredients/serves 4	
1kg/2lb mussels	75g/3 oz butter
Oil	400g/14 oz rice
3 cloves of garlic	Salt and pepper
½ small onion, chopped	Fish stock, or salted water

VENETO

Scrape the mussels and wash thoroughly in running water. Put them into a big pan with a little oil and half the garlic over a gentle heat. As the mussels open, remove them from their shells and set aside. Strain the cooking liquor and reserve. ☐ ☐ Soften the remaining garlic and the onion in half the butter and a little oil. Remove the garlic and pour in the rice. Season with salt and freshly ground pepper, adding the fish stock as necessary. Just before removing from the heat, stir in the mussels. Add the remaining butter and serve. *Photograph page 130*

RISOTTO CON LE TINCHE ALLA LOMBARDA

Tench risotto
For recipe, see p.124

RISOTTO ALLA TRASTEVERINA

*R*ICE WITH HAM AND CHICKEN LIVERS
For recipe, see p.121

RISOTTO ALLA PARMIGIANA
Parmesan risotto

EMILIA-
ROMAGNA

Ingredients/serves 4	400g/14 oz rice
1 small onion	6 tablespoons parmesan cheese
75g/3 oz butter	Salt
Olive oil	
1lt/2 pt meat stock, skimmed	

Thinly slice the onion and put in a pan with half the butter and 1 tablespoon oil and soften over a gentle heat without colouring. Add the rice and fry for a minute, then add a ladle of stock. When this has been absorbed, add another and repeat the process until half the stock has been used. Stir in half the remaining butter and 2 tablespoons parmesan. Continue adding the stock gradually. When the rice is cooked, season, add the remaining butter and parmesan and serve.

RISO CON ASPARAGI ALLA SICILIANA
Rice with asparagus

SICILY

Ingredients/serves 4	1 clove of garlic, chopped
500g/1lb asparagus	1 bunch of parsley, chopped
Oil	Salt
75g/3 oz fat bacon, chopped	300g/10 oz rice
1 onion, chopped	100g/4 oz caciocavallo cheese, diced

Clean the asparagus, cut off tough ends and boil for 12 minutes in salted water. Drain, cut off the tips and reserve the cooking liquor. In a pan, heat the oil and fry the bacon, onion, garlic and parsley. Pour on a little asparagus stock, season with salt and bring to the boil. Add the rice, adding more asparagus stock as it gets absorbed. When the rice is cooked, mix in the cheese and asparagus tips. *Photograph page 131*

RISO CON LE FAVE ALLA SICILIANA
Rice with lima beans

SICILY

Ingredients/serves 4	
75g/3 oz bacon	2 medium tomatoes, peeled, chopped and crushed with a fork
1 onion	
1 clove of garlic	Salt and pepper
½ stalk of celery	300g/10 oz shelled broad beans
1 bunch of parsley	400g/14 oz rice
Oil	Grated pecorino cheese

C hop the bacon, onion, garlic, celery and parsley finely together. Heat a little oil in a pan and cook the mixture gently, stirring. Add the tomatoes, season and cook for 10 minutes. ☐ ☐ Add the broad beans and 1.5lt/2½pt water. Bring to the boil and add the rice. Cook for 20 minutes until the rice is done and the consistency is thick and soupy. Sprinkle with pecorino to serve.

RISI E BISI
Rice and peas

VENETO

Ingredients/serves 4	
1.2kg/2¾ lb peas in the pod	Olive oil
2 tablespoons chopped parsley	1.5lt/2½ pt beef stock
1 onion	300g/10 oz rice
50g/2 oz lean pancetta bacon	5 tablespoons grated parmesan cheese
75g/3 oz butter	Salt and pepper

T his Venetian rice dish should be more like a thick soup than a risotto. Pod the peas and put in cold water. Wash and chop the parsley. Chop the onion and bacon, put in a pan with half the butter and 2 tablespoons oil, and cook until the onion has softened. Add the drained peas and a ladle of stock, stir and cook for 10 minutes. ☐ ☐ When the peas are half cooked, add the rest of the hot stock. Bring it back to the boil, add the rice and cook gently, stirring to prevent it from sticking to the bottom. Remove from the heat, add the remaining butter, stir in the parmesan, season to taste and serve.

RISOTTO CON LE COZZE ALLA GONDOLIERA

MUSSEL *RISOTTO*
For recipe, see p.125

RISO CON ASPARAGI ALLA SICILIANA

RICE WITH ASPARAGUS
For recipe, see p.128

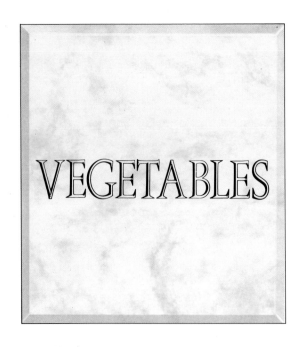

VEGETABLES

Fresh vegetables are the
delight of the Italian market
place. Fennel, baby peas,
artichokes, asparagus, broad
beans, chestnuts, funghi,
aubergines, peppers, courgettes
and tomatoes are all eaten in their
proper seasons, and often
make a complete course in
themselves.

RADICCHIO ROSSO DI TREVISO IN PADELLA

Fried radicchio

Ingredients/serves 4	Virgin olive oil
8 heads of Treviso radicchio	Salt and pepper

VENETO

Wash the radicchio well without removing the leaves and drain off as much water as possible. Then cut them into quarters from stem to tip and squeeze out more excess water (otherwise the oil will spit when heated). Put them on a plate and season with oil, salt and freshly ground pepper. ☐ ☐ Put a large frying pan on to heat and, when hot, put in the radicchio and cook briskly, turning over as soon as each side is cooked. Arrange on a serving dish. This method results in crisp radicchio — for softer radicchio, cook, covered, on a lower heat.

CAVOLO CON PANCETTA E PATATE

Cabbage with bacon and potatoes

Ingredients/serves 6	Salt and pepper
I curly cabbage (about Ikg/2lb)	Nutmeg
about 100g/4oz butter	600g/I¼ lb potatoes
200g/7oz smoked pancetta	Milk
bacon, chopped	2 egg yolks
Stock	

ABRUZZI-MOLISE

Preheat the oven to 180°C/350°F/Gas 4. Trim the cabbage and blanch in salted water for 10 minutes. Drain, squeeze and chop coarsely. Heat a little butter in a large pan, add the pancetta and cabbage, stir well and cover with stock. Season with salt, pepper and nutmeg and bring to the boil, then simmer over a moderate heat for 45 minutes. ☐ ☐ Boil the potatoes in another pan. Peel, then press through a sieve or blend while still hot. Put the purée in a small saucepan over a moderate heat, add half the butter and enough milk to give a soft, but not runny, consistency, season and mix in the egg yolks. ☐ ☐ Butter an ovenproof dish, put in the cabbage and pipe on the potato purée. Dot the top with the remaining butter and put in the oven for 10 minutes. Serve hot. *Photograph page 134*

*S*AVOY CABBAGE STUFFED WITH SCAMORZA CHEESE
For recipe, see p.136

CAVOLO CON PANCETTA E PATATE

*C*ABBAGE WITH BACON AND POTATOES
For recipe, see p.133

VERZA RIPIENA CON SCAMORZA ALLA NAPOLETANA

Savoy cabbage stuffed with scamorza cheese

CAMPANIA

Ingredients/serves 4	1 small onion, chopped
1 whole savoy cabbage, weighing 500g/1 lb	600g/1¼ lb tomatoes, peeled, deseeded and sieved
350g/12 oz cups scamorza cheese, thinly sliced (or use mozzarella)	Salt and pepper
	A few tablespoons grated parmesan cheese
Oil	

Preheat the oven to 180°C/350°F/Gas 4. Trim the cabbage stem and remove the outer leaves. Boil or steam it whole, until cooked but still firm. Allow to cool. Remove the leaves and put into 8 piles. Fill the top leaf in each pile with scamorza or mozzarella and roll up each one. □ □ Heat a little oil in a frying pan and fry the onion until soft. Add the tomato, season and cook over a moderate heat until very soft, being careful not to let it dry out. □ □ Put a layer of tomato in an ovenproof dish, arrange the cabbage rolls on top and pour the remaining sauce over. Sprinkle with parmesan, heat through in the oven for 10 minutes and serve hot. *Photograph page 134*

FAVE FRESCHE AL GUANCIALE

Broad beans with bacon

TUSCANY

Ingredients/serves 4	1 small onion, sliced
2kg/4½ lb broad beans in pods	1 cup stock
150g/5 oz pancetta, *or* bacon, diced	Salt and pepper
25g/1 oz lard *or* butter	

Pod the beans, if fresh, and put in a bowl of cold water. This will give about 1kg/2 lb beans. Put the bacon in a large pan, add the lard or butter and fry gently until the bacon fat runs. Then add the well-drained beans and the onion. Pour on the stock, season lightly, cover and cook briskly for about 40 minutes, stirring frequently. Transfer to a deep, preheated, serving dish. Serve garnished with triangles of toast.

CIPOLLINE NOVELLE ALLA ESCOFFIER
New onions Escoffier

VENETO

Ingredients/serves 4	
800g/1 ¾ lb new onions	1 teaspoon fennel seeds
Oil	40g/1 ½ oz sultanas soaked in
Salt and pepper	tepid water
1 bay leaf	1 glass dry white wine
A pinch of thyme	1 small glass Cognac

P eel the onions and boil for 5 minutes. Drain and dry. Heat some oil in a pan, add the onions, season and fry gently until golden brown, being careful not to allow them to burn. Add the bay leaf, thyme, fennel seeds and sultanas, and pour on the wine and Cognac. Bring to the boil, cover and cook for another 5 minutes. Remove from the heat, allow to cool and serve.

Photograph page 139

ZUCCHINI ALLA PAESANA
Country-style courgettes

ABRUZZI-
MOLISE

Ingredients/serves 4	
500g/1 lb courgettes	1 onion, sliced
1 egg	500g/1 lb tomatoes, peeled and
Salt and pepper	deseeded
75g/3 oz breadcrumbs	½ tablespoon sugar
Knob of butter	100g/4 oz grated parmesan
Oil	1 tablespoon chopped basil
	4 mint leaves, chopped

P reheat the oven to 180°C/350°F/Gas 4. Cut the ends off the courgettes and cut lengthwise. Beat the egg with a little salt. Dip the courgettes in the egg, and then in breadcrumbs. Melt a little butter in a pan with some oil and fry the courgettes until golden. Drain on absorbent kitchen paper. ☐ ☐ Heat 4 tablespoons oil in a pan and cook the onion for 5 minutes. Add the tomatoes, sugar, salt and pepper, then cover and cook on a medium heat for 30 minutes, stirring occasionally. ☐ ☐ Butter a baking dish, put in a layer of courgettes, cover with a little sauce, sprinkle with parmesan, basil and mint, and continue the layers like this until all the ingredients have been used up. End with the sauce and put in the oven for 15 minutes. ☐ ☐ This dish can be served straight away, but is also delicious lukewarm or cold.

*A*UBERGINES *WITH TOMATOES*
For recipe, see p.144

*N*EW *ONIONS ESCOFFIER*
For recipe, see p.137

FONDI DI CARCIOFI ALLA FIORENTINA

Artichoke hearts with spinach

TUSCANY

Ingredients/serves 4	For the sauce
8 artichoke hearts	50g/2oz butter
Juice of 1 lemon	2 tablespoons flour
Olive oil	150ml/$\frac{1}{4}$ pt milk
Flour	150ml/$\frac{1}{4}$pt cream
600g/ 1 $\frac{1}{4}$ lb spinach	Salt and pepper
Salt and pepper	Nutmeg
50g/2oz butter	4 tablespoons grated
3 tablespoons parmesan cheese	emmenthal cheese
3 tablespoons breadcrumbs	

P reheat the oven to 190°C/375°F/Gas 5. Steam or boil the artichoke hearts in water acidulated with a little lemon juice, to which you have added 1 tablespoon oil and 1 teaspoon flour. Meanwhile trim and wash the spinach in several changes of water, then cook in the water clinging to the leaves, salting lightly. When cooked, rinse in cold water and squeeze dry. Melt half the butter in a pan, add the spinach, season and let it absorb the butter over a gentle heat, then stir in 1 tablespoon parmesan. ☐ ☐ For the sauce, melt the butter in a small pan and add the flour, blending well with a wooden spoon to avoid lumps forming. Add the milk and cream, season and add a pinch of nutmeg. Cook, stirring, until the sauce has thickened and is simmering. Stir in the cheese and remove from the heat. ☐ ☐ Grease a large ovenproof dish. Cut a sliver off the bottom of each artichoke heart so that they stand upright and arrange them in the dish. Divide the spinach between them, making little heaps on top. Pour over the sauce, sprinkle on the remaining parmesan and breadcrumbs and dot on the remaining butter. Put into the oven for about 10 minutes until golden on top. Serve at once.

ASPARAGI ALLA MILANESE

Asparagus with eggs and cheese

Ingredients/serves 4	100g/4oz butter
1.5kg/3 lb asparagus (purple-tipped)	3 tablespoons parmesan cheese
4 eggs	

LOMBARDY

C lean the asparagus and poach or steam them. Drain and arrange on a heated serving dish. Fry the eggs in about half the butter. Heat the remaining butter separately. Sprinkle the parmesan on the asparagus, put the just-set eggs carefully on top, then trickle on the melted butter. Serve at once.

POLPETTONE DI BIETOLE ALLA LIGURE

Beets with cream and mushrooms

Ingredients/serves 4	2 eggs
75g/3oz butter	3 tablespoons cream
Oil	2 tablespoons grated parmesan cheese
350g/12oz fresh mushrooms, sliced	Salt and pepper
1 clove of garlic, chopped	Breadcrumbs
1.5kg/3lb beets, cooked, peeled and chopped	

LIGURIA

P reheat the oven to 180°C/350°F/Gas 4. Melt the butter with a little oil in a frying pan, add the mushrooms and garlic and fry until soft. Stir in the beets and cook gently so that the flavours mingle. ☐
☐ Put the eggs in a bowl with the cream and parmesan and beat together well. Season. Tip the beets into the bowl and stir well to coat in the egg mixture. ☐ ☐ Grease an ovenproof dish, sprinkle with breadcrumbs and fill with the beet mixture, levelling off the top. Sprinkle with breadcrumbs again, dribble a little oil over the top and cook in the oven until golden.

SPINACI ALLA ROMANO

SPINACH ROMAN STYLE
For recipe, see p.145

RUSTICANA ALLA PIACENTINA

COUNTRY-STYLE PEPPERS AND TOMATOES
For recipe, see p.145

143

PORRI CON BESCIAMELLA

Leeks in béchamel sauce

EMILIA-
ROMAGNA

Ingredients/serves 4	75g/3oz cooked ham, cut in
600g/1¼ lb leeks	strips
Salt	200ml/⅓pt béchamel sauce
25g/1oz butter	with 1 egg yolk added
	50g/2oz grated gruyère

P reheat the oven to 200°C/400°F/Gas 6. Trim the leeks, discarding the green part, and wash well. Boil in lightly salted water, drain and arrange in an ovenproof dish. Dot with butter, cover with the ham and pour over the béchamel sauce. Sprinkle on the gruyère and put in the oven until golden brown.

MELANZANE AL POMODORI

Aubergine with tomatoes

CALABRIA

Ingredients/serves 4	Salt and pepper
4 large aubergines	1¼ cups deseeded and chopped
Oil	tomatoes
2 cloves of garlic, crushed	

C ut off ends of aubergines, wash and cut them into chunks without removing peel. Heat some oil in a pan and fry garlic until soft. Add aubergines and season. Cook gently for 10 minutes. Add tomato and continue to cook for 20 minutes over a low heat until aubergines are done. Pile into a dish and serve.   *Photograph page 139*

SPINACI ALLA ROMANA
Spinach Roman style

Ingredients/serves 4	75g/3oz pine nuts
1kg/2 lb spinach	Salt
Oil	75g/3oz sultanas, soaked until
1 clove of garlic, crushed	plump
75g/3oz bacon, thinly-sliced	Knob of butter

LAZIO, UMBRIA AND THE MARCHES

Wash the spinach, discarding tough stalks and discoloured leaves. Cook gently in the water clinging to it, drain and squeeze out. Heat a little oil in a pan, add the garlic, ham and spinach, and cook gently, stirring. After a few minutes, add the pine nuts and sultanas. Remove from the heat, put in a serving dish with a knob of butter and serve.

Photograph page 142

RUSTICANA ALLA PIACENTINA
Country-style peppers and tomatoes

Ingredients/serves 4	500g/1 lb tomatoes, skinned,
50g/2oz butter	deseeded and chopped
Oil	Salt
500g/1 lb spring onions	4 hard-boiled eggs, chopped
4 large green or yellow	
peppers, cut into julienne strips	

EMILIA-ROMAGNA

Heat the butter with some oil in a pan and fry the onions and peppers until half cooked. If preferred, the peppers can be charred and skinned first. Then add the tomatoes, season, add a little tepid water and cook over a moderate heat, stirring occasionally. As soon as the peppers are cooked, stir in the egg and serve.

Photograph page 143

FISH

Because the Italians are firm believers in using only fresh local produce, you will be unlikely to find seafood in Italy at any distance from the coast. Fish — whether from sea or rivers — is perhaps at its best simply cooked with butter or olive oil, a few leaves of sage and served with a wedge of lemon.

Trota Salmonata con Agliata alla Ligure
Salmon trout with aïoli

LIGURIA

Ingredients/serves 4	Salt and pepper
1 salmon trout weighing 1kg/2lb	4 cloves of garlic
2 small carrots, chopped	2 slices crustless white
1 stalk of celery, chopped	bread, softened in vinegar
2 small onions, chopped	1 glass oil
1 tablespoon chopped parsley	Lemon wedges
3 medium potatoes,	50g/2oz butter, melted
peeled and sliced	

C lean and wash the trout, put in a fish kettle or a pan that it will fit and cover with a court bouillon made from 1.5lt/2pt water, the carrots, celery, onions and parsley. Bring gently to the boil and simmer for 12 minutes. Boil the potatoes in salted water. In a mortar, pound the garlic with the bread, season and gradually add the oil, as if you were making mayonnaise. ☐ ☐ Drain the trout, put on a dish and surround with lemon wedges. Serve with the potatoes, dribbled with melted butter, and hand the aïoli separately. *Photograph page 148*

Razza con Burro di Acciughe
Skate with anchovy butter

CAMPANIA

Ingredients/serves 4	Salt and pepper
1kg/2 lb skate	25g/1 oz capers in vinegar
2 small carrots, chopped	25g/1 oz pickled gherkins, sliced
1 stalk of celery, chopped	1 tablespoon chopped parsley
2 small onions, chopped	Squeeze of lemon juice
75g/3oz butter	5 anchovies soaked in milk
40g/1½oz flour	

P oach the skate and onion in court a bouillon made of 600ml/1pt water which has previously been bought to the boil with the carrots, celery and onions. When cooked, transfer the fish to a serving platter and keep warm. Melt half the butter, blend in the flour and a little fish liquor. Return it to the pan, season and simmer, stirring, for 7-8 minutes until the sauce has thickened and is smooth and velvety. Add the capers, gherkins, parsley and lemon juice. Drain the anchovies and pound with the remaining butter. Blend the anchovy butter into the sauce. Heat through, pour over the skate and serve. *Photograph page 148*

SALMON TROUT WITH AÏOLI
For recipe, see p.147

RAZZA CON BURRO DI ACCIUGHE

SKATE WITH ANCHOVY BUTTER
For recipe, see p.147

SARDE FRITTE ALLA LIGURE
Fried stuffed sardines

LIGURIA

Ingredients/serves 4	
16 sardines	50g/2 oz grated parmesan cheese
Olive oil	1 clove of garlic, crushed
25g/1oz dried mushrooms, softened in water	1 teaspoon chopped marjoram
100g/4 oz fresh breadcrumbs, softened in a little milk and squeezed	A pinch of oregano
	4 eggs
	Salt and pepper
	Flour
	Stale breadcrumbs (not the crust)

Clean the sardines, removing the heads and tails. Open them out, remove the bones, wash and dry on a cloth. Heat a little olive oil in a frying pan, chop the mushrooms finely and fry gently for a few minutes. Transfer them to a dish and add the fresh breadcrumbs, parmesan, garlic, marjoram, oregano, 2 of the eggs and a pinch of salt. ☐ ☐ Stuff the sardines with this mixture, then close them up. Dip them first into flour, then into seasoned beaten egg, then into stale breadcrumbs. Fry in hot oil and serve immediately. *Photograph page 152*

SARDE A BECCAFICU CATANESE
Baked stuffed sardines

CALABRIA

Ingredients/serves 4	
16 sardines	Flour
2 tablespoons vinegar	2 eggs, beaten
Salt and pepper	Breadcrumbs
100g/4 oz chopped parsley and garlic mixed with grated parmesan cheese	Olive oil
	2 lemons

Preheat the oven to 190°C/375°F/Gas 5. Clean the sardines, removing the heads and tails, open them out without splitting them and remove the bones. Wash and dry them. Arrange on a big dish, sprinkle with vinegar, season and stuff each one with the parsley, garlic and cheese mixture. Close the fish up again, pressing down well, dip them in flour, in the beaten egg and then in breadcrumbs. ☐ ☐ Put the sardines in a greased overproof dish, sprinkle with oil and put in the oven for 25-30 minutes. Serve with lemon wedges.

Sgombri alla Calabrese
Mackerel with anchovy butter

Ingredients/serves 4	
2 mackerel, 500g/1 lb each	40g/1½ oz anchovy paste
Olive oil	40g/1½oz butter
Salt and pepper	1 tablespoon chopped parsley
	Lemon juice to taste

CALABRIA

Clean the mackerel, remove the heads, open them out, take out the backbone and wash them. Sprinkle with oil, grill or barbeque over wood, and season well. For the anchovy butter, mix together the remaining ingredients. Hand the anchovy butter separately.

Stoccafisso alla Siciliana
Dried cod Sicilian style

Ingredients/serves 4	
800g/1¾ lb dried cod, already soaked	Salt and pepper
	200g/7 oz ripe olives, pitted
Olive oil	40g/1½ oz capers
1 small onion, chopped	40g/1½ oz sultanas, soaked
1 large clove of garlic, chopped	40g/1½ oz pine nuts
½ glass white wine	3 medium-sized potatoes, peeled and sliced
600g/1¼ lb tomato flesh	

SICILY

Preheat the oven to 190°C/375°F/Gas 5. Remove the bones and skin from the cod and cut the flesh into cubes. Heat some oil in a pan, fry the onion and garlic and add the fish. Cook for a minute then add the wine. When it has reduced, add the tomato and enough water to cover the fish. Season with salt and freshly ground black pepper. □ □ Bring to the boil, cover and put in the oven for an hour. Add the potatoes, olives, capers, sultanas, and pine nuts. Continue cooking until the potatoes are done, then serve immediately. *Photograph page 152*

SARDE FRITTE ALLA LIGURE

*F*RIED *STUFFED SARDINES*
For recipe, see p.150

STOCCAFISSO ALLA SICILIANA

*D*RIED *COD SICILIAN STYLE*
For recipe, see p.151

TOTANI O CALAMARI IN ZIMINO ALLA GENOVESE

Squid or calamari in a spicy sauce

LIGURIA

Ingredients/serves 4	Olive oil
600g/1 ¼ lb small squid	½ glass dry white wine
2 tablespoons chopped parsley	1 tablespoon tomato paste
2 cloves of garlic	Salt and pepper
1 onion	1 kg/2 lb fresh beets
1 stalk of celery	

Clean the squid and cut into strips, then wash and drain. Prepare and chop together the parsley, 1 clove of garlic, the onion and celery. Put them in a large frying pan with half a glass of oil over a moderate heat and fry for a few minutes. Add the squid and continue to fry, gradually adding the white wine. When it has evaporated add the tomato paste, diluted in a little water. Season and cook gently, stirring occasionally. ☐ ☐ Meanwhile trim the beets, wash well and cut into small pieces. Heat 4 tablespoons oil in a pan and add the remaining garlic, crushed. Cook until it begins to brown. Then add the beets, season well, stir, cover the pan and cook gently for 10 minutes. Add the squid and cook for a further 10 minutes. Serve on a platter with triangles of toast.

SOGLIOLE ALL'ERBA SALVIA
Sole with sage

Ingredients/serves 4	2 eggs, beaten
8 sole fillets	Breadcrumbs
A little flour	Oil
Salt and pepper	A few sage leaves

VENETO

Dip the sole fillets in flour, then in seasoned beaten egg, then in breadcrumbs, pressing them well on with your fingers. Fry them in plenty of hot oil, together with the sage. When golden brown, remove and drain on absorbent paper and sprinkle with salt. Arrange on a serving dish and serve with boiled potatoes. *Photograph page 156*

SCAMPI GRIGLIATA
Grilled scampi

Ingredients/serves 4	Salt and pepper
1 kg/2lb scampi	100g/4 oz butter
Olive oil	2 cloves of garlic, crushed

VENETO

Peel the scampi, wash and dry. Lay them in a dish and pour over enough olive oil to coat. Season well and leave, covered, to marinate for an hour, stirring occasionally. □ □ Melt the butter with the garlic in a small saucepan over a low heat, stirring. Remove from the heat and allow the flavours to mingle. □ □ Meanwhile, thread the scampi onto wooden skewers. Brush with oil from the marinade and put under a hot grill for 15-20 minutes, turning once. They should be nicely browned. Remove the scampi from the skewers and arrange them on a serving dish. Hand the garlic butter separately. *Photograph page 156*

SOLE WITH SAGE
For recipe, see p.155

SCAMPI GRIGLIATA

BROILED JUMBO SHRIMP
For recipe, see p.155

TRIGLIE AL PROSCIUTTO
Red mullet with ham

LAZIO, UMBRIA
AND
THE MARCHES

Ingredients/serves 4	1 clove garlic
12 small red mullet	Olive oil
Salt and pepper	50g/2 oz breadcrumbs
12 slices of prosciutto	1 tablespoon chopped parsley
4 ripe tomatoes	Juice of ½ lemon

P repare and wash the mullet, dry and season with salt. Wrap each one in a slice of prosciutto. Blanch the tomatoes for 1 minute, peel, deseed and slice. Cook the garlic for 5 minutes in a pan with the oil. Add the mullet and cook for 2-3 minutes on each side, turning them gently. Add the tomatoes, sprinkle with breadcrumbs, season and cook over a low heat for 10 minutes. Sprinkle with parsley and lemon juice. Put the mullet on a dish and serve. *Photograph page 161*

TRIGLIE ALLA LIVORNESE
Red mullet Livorno style

TUSCANY

Ingredients/serves 4	4 red mullet
500g/1 lb ripe tomatoes	4 tablespoons chopped
25g/1 oz butter	parsley
Olive oil	1 stalk of celery
A few basil leaves	1 clove garlic
Salt and pepper	Flour

W ash and sieve or blend the tomatoes. In a small pan, heat the butter, 2 tablespoons oil and the basil, then add the tomatoes, season and cook gently for 30 minutes. Meanwhile, descale the fish and remove the fins, gut them; wash and drain them well. ☐ ☐ Trim and wash the parsley and celery and chop finely together with the clove of garlic. Put this, together with half a glass of oil, into a pan which you can bring to the table. Fry for a few minutes. ☐ ☐ Lightly flour the fish and brown on one side. Remove from the heat and very carefully (mullet are fragile) turn them over. Put them back on the heat. Pour over the tomato sauce and cook for about 10 minutes. Serve them in the pan.

Photograph page 160

POLPI AFFOGATI ALLA LUCIANA
Octopus in tomato sauce

APULIA

Ingredients/serves 4	2 medium tomatoes, skinned
2 rock octopuses	and chopped
(500g/1 lb each)	1 red chilli
Salt	1 glass oil
2 tablespoons chopped parsley	Lemon wedges

Clean the octopuses. Peel off the skin and beat them to tenderize. Wash and put them in a flameproof earthenware dish. Season with salt and add the parsley, tomatoes, chilli and oil. Cover the dish tightly with 2 sheets of waxed paper, and secure with the lid or with string. Cook over a very low heat for about 2 hours. □ □ Remove the chilli, cut the octopuses into pieces and serve in the cooking dish. Accompany with lemon wedges.

SEPPIE AI PISELLI
Squid with peas

VENETO

Ingredients/serves 4	1½ lb peas in their pods
A handful of basil leaves	½ glass dry white wine
A large bunch of parsley	3 cups ripe tomatoes, skinned,
1 stalk of celery	deseeded and chopped
1 clove of garlic	1 bayleaf
1 onion	Salt and pepper
2 lb squid	

Chop together the basil, celery, garlic and onion. Clean the squid. Remove the mouth and eyes. Wash thoroughly and peel away the outer membranes. Remove the cuttlefish bone. Slice the body and the tentacles. Pod the peas into a saucepan of cold water. □ □ Put the butter in a flameproof casserole and set over heat to melt. Add the chopped vegetables and cook until soft. Stir in the squid and pour over the white wine. Cook for a few minutes until the wine has almost evaporated. Stir in the tomatoes and peas. Add the bayleaf and season with salt and pepper. Cover and cook over a moderate flame for about 1 hour, stirring occasionally to ensure that sauce does not stick to bottom of pan. Serve hot with rice, potatoes or polenta.

TRIGLIE ALLA LIVORNESE

RED MULLET LIVORNO STYLE
For recipe, see p.158

TRIGLIE AL PROSCIUTTO

RED MULLET WITH HAM
For recipe, se p.158

POULTRY AND GAME

Poultry and game, for Italians who live in the country or in the poorer south, are virtually free foods. Many families have chickens scratching about in their back yards and hunting is a national pastime, be it for pheasant, quail, rabbit, hare or even wild boar.

POLLO RIPIENO AI CARCIOFI
Chicken stuffed with artichokes

EMILIA-
ROMAGNA

Ingredients/serves 4	4 artichoke hearts
I clove of garlic	1/2 lemon, sliced
A sprig of rosemary	4 sage leaves
25g/I oz butter, softened	2 tablespoons olive oil
Salt and pepper	I glass dry white wine
I chicken weighing about 1.5kg/3 lb	

Preheat the oven to 180°C/350°F/Gas 4. Crush the garlic and rosemary. Put in a bowl with the butter and seasoning and mix with a wooden spoon until finely creamed. Wash and dry the chicken and stuff with the artichoke hearts and lemon. Sew up the opening with cotton thread. □ □ Skewer the chicken together with a thin skewer, putting the sage leaves under the wings and thighs. Rub the butter mixture all over the chicken, then season well. Put in a baking tin or dish and pour the oil over. Cook in the oven for 1 1/2 hours, turning frequently. Remove from the oven when golden brown. Untie the chicken, transfer to a serving plate and cut into pieces. Arrange the artichoke hearts round it, and discard the lemon. Pour the wine into the pan and heat the sauce over a low flame, stirring well. Pour the sauce over the chicken and serve at once.

Photograph page 165

POLLO CON PEPERONATA
Chicken with peperonata

APULIA

Ingredients/serves 4	3 peppers, deseeded and cut into strips
4 tablespoons oil	
25g/I oz butter	I onion, sliced
I chicken weighing about I kg/ 2 lb, jointed	Salt and pepper
	Stock
1/2 glass dry white wine	2 tablespoons chopped basil
500g/I lb ripe tomatoes, skinned	

Heat the oil and butter together in a pan and brown the chicken pieces for 5 minutes. Pour over the wine and boil to reduce slightly. Add the vegetables, season, add stock and cook over a low heat for 1 1/2 hours. Sprinkle with basil and serve. *Photograph page 165*

CHICKEN STUFFED WITH ARTICHOKES
For recipe, see p.163

POLLO CON PEPERONATA

CHICKEN WITH PEPERONATA
For recipe, see p.163

165

FILETTI DI TACCHINO ALLA BOLOGNESE

Turkey breasts Bologna style

EMILIA-
ROMAGNA

Ingredients/serves 4	Salt and pepper
600g/1¼ lb turkey breasts, sliced	About 200ml/⅓pt meat stock
100g/4oz butter	½ teaspoon meat extract
Flour	1 white truffle (optional)
Dry marsala	4 tablespoons parmesan cheese

Beat the turkey slices flat. Choose a pan large enough to accommodate them in one layer. Heat half the butter in pan until it browns. Flour the turkey slices and fry briskly on both sides. Sprinkle on a few tablespoons of marsala, season and cook until the marsala has evaporated. Remove the meat with a slotted spoon. ☐ ☐ Pour half the stock into a pan and stir in the meat extract. Bring to the boil and add turkey breasts, turning to let them absorb the flavour. Cook over a low heat for a few minutes. Clean the truffle if using, and wash it in a little white wine. Slice finely. ☐ ☐ Preheat the oven to 190°C/375°F/Gas 5. Put the turkey in a greased ovenproof dish. Add a little stock to the sauce left in the pan and cook over a high flame, stirring well to dissolve any sediment left at the bottom. Cover the turkey with truffle slices, sprinkle with parmesan, add the sauce from the pan, and the remaining butter. Cover and put in the oven until the cheese melts. Serve with creamed potatoes, asparagus tips, buttered spinach or glazed onions.

ANITRA ALL'ACCIUGA

Duck with anchovies

ABRUZZI-
MOLISE

Ingredients/serves 4	A few slices of ginger
10 anchovy fillets	100g/4 oz pitted green olives
8 cloves of garlic	Oil
1 onion, sliced	1 duck, jointed
1 carrot, sliced	Salt
1 stalk of celery, sliced	A little stock

Put the anchovies, garlic, vegetables, ginger and olives into a large saucepan. Coat with a few tablespoons of oil and fry for 5 minutes. Add the duck joints to the pan with a very little salt (the anchovies will already be salty) and brown on a high heat. Cover and then cook over a moderate heat for 45 minutes, adding a little stock as necessary to prevent the duck from drying out. *Photograph page 168*

FAGIANO ARROSTO CON UVA E NOCI
Roast pheasant with grapes and walnuts

Ingredients/serves 4	
1 pheasant	12 walnuts, shelled
4 slices pancetta bacon	2 tablespoons brandy
1 kg/2 lb white grapes	Salt and pepper
Small carton soured cream	25g/1 oz butter

LAZIO, UMBRIA AND THE MARCHES

Wrap the pheasant in the pancetta slices and secure with a thin skewer. Keep aside a quarter of the grapes and press the rest through a sieve or process in a blender. Drain off the juice and reserve. Put the pheasant in a pan, add the cream, walnuts, brandy, grape juice and a pinch of salt and pepper to taste. Cover and cook over a low heat for an hour, stirring frequently. □ □ Preheat the oven to 250°C/475°F/Gas 9. Remove the pheasant from the pan and take off the pancetta slices. Line a roasting tin with foil and put the pheasant in it. Cook for 10 minutes until golden brown. Pour the cooking juices into a saucepan, remove the nuts and reduce to about 200ml/⅓ pt over a high flame. Add the butter and stir until it melts. Put the pheasant on a serving dish and surround with walnuts and reserve grapes. Pour the boiling gravy sauce over the pheasant and serve at once.

CONIGLIO CON PEPERONI
Rabbit with peppers

Ingredients/serves 4	
1 rabbit, jointed	Salt and pepper
50g/2 oz butter	Stock
4 tablespoons oil	4 peppers, sliced
A sprig of rosemary	4 anchovy fillets, chopped
1 bay leaf	2 cloves of garlic, crushed
	2 tablespoons vinegar

APULIA

Brown the rabbit joints in a pan with half the butter and half the oil, the rosemary and bay leaf. Season and cook on a low heat for 1½ hours, adding stock as necessary to keep it moist. □ □ In another saucepan, heat the remaining butter and oil and add the peppers, anchovies, garlic and vinegar. Season and cook gently for 20 minutes. Add the pepper sauce to the rabbit, let the flavours mingle for 5 minutes and then serve. Photograph page 169

ANITRA ALL'ACCIUGA

DUCK WITH ANCHOVIES
For recipe, see p.166

CONIGLIO CON PEPERONI

*R*ABBIT WITH PEPPERS
For recipe, see p.167

QUAGLIE CON PANCETTA
Quail with pancetta bacon

LAZIO, UMBRIA AND THE MARCHES

Ingredients/serves 4	3 medium potatoes
8 plump quails	4 slices lean smoked pancetta,
Salt and pepper	blanched
8 thin rashers of bacon	A little stock
100g/4oz butter	

C lean the quails, season, truss with a skewer and wrap the bacon slices round them, securing with a thread. Heat half the butter in a pan, put in the quail and cook, turning occasionally. Peel the potatoes, slice and fry until browned in the remaining butter with a pinch of salt. Drain the quails, reserving the juices, arrange on a dish and garnish with the fried potatoes and pancetta. ☐ ☐ Add a few tablespoons of stock to the cooking juices in the pan, using a wooden spoon to scrape off the sediment sticking to the bottom. Heat through, stirring, then pour the sauce onto the quail and serve.

QUAGLIE AL BRANDY ALLA ROMANA
Quail in brandy with peas

LAZIO, UMBRIA AND THE MARCHES

Ingredients/serves 4	350g/12oz shelled peas
8 plump quails	Stock
100g/4oz butter	Salt and freshly ground pepper
3 small glasses brandy	250g/8oz prosciutto, cut into
½ onion, chopped	strips

C lean the quails and truss them. Heat half the butter in a pan, put in the quails and cook briskly for 15 minutes. Moisten with brandy and continue to cook until it has almost completely evaporated. Transfer the quails to a serving dish with their cooking juices, untie and keep hot. ☐ ☐ In a separate pan, fry the onion in the remaining butter, add the peas and a little stock, season and cook, covered, until tender. Just before removing the peas from the heat, add the prosciutto. Garnish the quails with the peas and ham and serve. *Photograph page 172*

INSALATA DI POLLO E RISO

Chicken and rice salad

Ingredients/serves 4	A few tomatoes
350g/12oz cold cooked rice	A few hearty lettuce leaves
300g/10oz cooked chicken, sliced	Oil
	Juice of 1 lemon
100g/4oz salted tongue, diced	3 tablespoons double cream
75g/3oz truffle (optional)	Salt and pepper
1 tablespoon coarsely chopped basil	

PIEDMONT

Mix the rice, chicken, tongue and truffle together in a bowl. Sprinkle on the basil, decorate the salad with tomato and lettuce and pour over the dressing made by mixing together equal quantities of oil, lemon juice and cream, seasoned with salt and pepper.

Photograph page 173

POLLO FRITTO ALLA TOSCANA

Tuscan fried chicken

Ingredients/serves 4	2-3 tablespoons olive oil
1 chicken weighing about 1.5kg/3½ lb	Salt and pepper
	Oil
A large bunch of parsley, chopped	Flour
	2 eggs, beaten
Juice of 1 lemon	

TUSCANY

Cut the chicken into regular-sized cubes. Put it in a casserole and sprinkle with parsley and lemon juice. Pour over the olive oil and season with salt and pepper. Turn the chicken cubes in the marinade and leave for about 2 hours. ☐ ☐ 20 minutes before you are ready to eat, heat some oil for frying in a large pan. Remove the chicken from the marinade, dust with flour and coat with beaten egg. When the oil is very hot, add the chicken cubes and fry over a moderate heat for about 15 minutes until crisp and golden. ☐ ☐ Remove the chicken with a slotted spoon and drain on absorbent paper. Season again with salt and serve very hot.

QUAGLIE CON PANCETTA

QUAIL WITH PANCETTA BACON
For recipe, see p.170

INSALATA DI POLLO E RISO

CHICKEN AND RICE SALAD
For recipe, see p.171

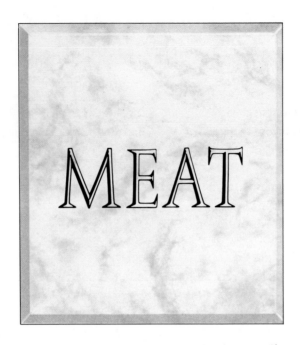

MEAT

Meat was a luxury in Italy until after the Second World War. The Italians are very fond of suckling pig, lamb and kid roasted on a spit over an open wood fire, but their favourite meat is probably veal. Some say that the word for veal — vitello — even gave the country its name.

ROGNONE DI VITELLO AL TEGAME CON FUNGHI

Veal kidneys with mushrooms

Ingredients/serves 4	2 veal kidneys, weighing 250g/
I small onion, chopped	8oz each, fat and skin removed
I clove of garlic, crushed	Butter
Oil	Chopped parsley
4 mushrooms, sliced	2 slices bread
Salt and pepper	

TUSCANY

Fry the onion and garlic in the oil, add the mushrooms, season with salt and pepper and cook through on a moderate heat. In another pan, sauté the kidneys in half the butter and a few tablespoons of oil until done. Season, add the mushrooms and cook for a few moments. Put on a serving dish, sprinkle with parsley and garnish with bread cut into triangles and fried in the remaining butter and a little oil. *Photograph page 177*

VITELLO CON PROSCIUTTO ALLA TOSCANA

Tuscan veal with ham

Ingredients/serves 4	100g/4oz prosciutto, cut into
I kg/2 lb best end of veal	strips
Salt and pepper	I glass Tuscan red wine
Flour	2 medium potatoes, boiled
40g/1½oz butter	I clove of garlic, crushed
Oil	Grated rind of I lemon
I onion, chopped	Nutmeg

TUSCANY

Roll and skewer the meat. Season and flour lightly. Melt the butter in a flameproof casserole, add a little oil and brown the meat. Stir in the onion and prosciutto, pour in the wine and reduce over a brisk heat until it has almost evaporated. Cover the meat with water and continue to cook, stirring occasionally. □ □ Just before the veal is done, add the potatoes and stir in the garlic, lemon rind and a pinch of nutmeg, and let the flavours mingle. Put the meat on a serving dish, pour over the cooking juices, garnish with potatoes and serve. *Photograph page 177*

ROGNONE DI VITELLO AL TEGAME CON FUNGHI

*V*EAL *KIDNEYS WITH MUSHROOMS*
For recipe, see p.175

VITELLO CON PROSCIUTTO ALLA TOSCANA

*T*USCAN *VEAL WITH HAM*
For recipe, see p.175

POLPETTE ALLA GENOVESE
Genoese meatballs

LIGURIA

Ingredients/serves 4	2 tablespoons grated parmesan
400g/14oz cooked veal, minced	Salt and pepper
	Nutmeg
50g/2oz breadcrumbs, soaked in stock or milk and squeezed	1 egg, beaten
	A little flour
1 clove of garlic, crushed	Oil or oil and lard, for deep-frying
1 bunch of parsley, chopped	
A few marjoram leaves	
40g/1½oz dried mushrooms, soaked, drained and chopped	

I n a bowl, mix the veal, bread, garlic, parsley, marjoram, mushrooms and cheese. Season with salt, pepper and nutmeg and bind with the egg, stirring well. Form the mixture into balls, flatten slightly and dip in flour. Fry until golden brown in plenty of oil or oil and lard, lower the heat and cook through. Serve hot.   *Photograph page 180*

COSTOLETTINE DI VITELLO ALLA VALDOSTANA
Veal cutlets with bacon and cheese

VENETO

Ingredients/serves 4	A sprig of rosemary
4 veal cutlets	A little brandy
Salt	4 slices smoked pancetta (or bacon)
1 egg, beaten	
Soft breadcrumbs	4 slices fontina cheese
75g/3 oz butter	

F latten the cutlets a little, exposing the bone. Salt them, dip in beaten egg and coat with breadcrumbs, pressing them well on. Heat the butter in a pan until foaming and fry the cutlets gently until cooked.
☐ ☐ Grease a large casserole dish, lay the cutlets on the bottom and sprinkle with a few finely chopped rosemary leaves. Sprinkle on a few drops of brandy, then cover each cutlet with one slice of pancetta and one slice of fontina. Put in a hot oven for a few minutes until the cheese has half-melted. Serve very hot.

ROTOLO DI VITELLO RIPIENO

Stuffed shoulder of veal

Ingredients/serves 4	1 glass dry white wine
1 small onion, sliced	4 tablespoons grated parmesan
150g/5oz fresh sausage, sliced	cheese
75g/3oz butter	800g/1¾ lb shoulder of veal in
200g/7oz rice	one piece
Salt and pepper	A sprig of rosemary
1lt/2pt boiling stock	Oil
1 bunch parsley, chopped	

LOMBARDY

Preheat the oven to 190°C/375°F/Gas 5. ☐ ☐ Fry the onion and sausage in half the butter. Add the rice, season, then cook, adding the boiling stock gradually and stirring frequently. When the rice is nearly cooked, add the parsley and half the wine and leave the risotto on the heat until the wine has completely evaporated. Sprinkle on the parmesan cheese. ☐ ☐ Flatten out the veal, season and spread the risotto onto it. Roll up the meat, insert the rosemary, secure with a skewer and put in a pan with the remaining butter and a few tablespoons oil. Put in the oven and brown, turning frequently. ☐ ☐ After 30 minutes, pour over the remaining wine and cook for another hour. Remove from the oven, slice and serve immediately.

SALTIMBOCCA ALLA ROMANA

Veal escalopes with ham

Ingredients/serves 4	8 sage leaves
8 slices of best end of veal	A little flour
Salt and pepper	75g/3 oz butter
8 slices prosciutto	1 glass dry white wine

**LAZIO, UMBRIA
AND
THE MARCHES**

Flatten the meat into thick wedge shapes, season and cover each wedge with a slice of prosciutto and a sage leaf. Fold each one in half and secure with a skewer. Flour lightly. Heat 60g/2½ oz butter in a pan and fry the saltimbocca on a brisk heat until brown all over and cooked. ☐ ☐ Remove with a slotted spoon and arrange on a serving dish. Add the wine to the cooking juices and reduce almost completely. Add the remaining butter and pour the hot sauce over the saltimbocca. Serve at once. *Photograph page 180*

POLPETTE ALLA GENOVESE

GENOESE MEATBALLS
For recipe, see p.178

SALTIMBOCCA ALLA ROMANA

VEAL ESCALOPES WITH HAM
For recipe, see p.179

COSTOLETTE DI VITELLO ALLA PALERMITANO

Veal cutlets with pecorino

SICILY

Ingredients/serves 4	2 eggs, beaten
4 veal cutlets	50g/2 oz pecorino cheese,
Wine vinegar	grated
Salt and pepper	Breadcrumbs
3 cloves of garlic, crushed	Oil
A bunch of parsley	

Beat the cutlets a little and expose the bone with a knife. Put on a plate, sprinkle on a little good quality wine vinegar and leave to marinate for an hour or so. Drain, dry and season with salt and pepper. Mix the garlic and parsley into the beaten egg, and mix the pecorino with the breadcrumbs. Dip the cutlets first into the egg, then into the breadcrumbs, pressing well on so that the coating sticks. Fry in hot oil, browning both sides. Drain when crisp and serve.

OSSIBUCHI ALLA MILANESE

Braised veal Milan-style

LOMBARDY

Ingredients/serves 4	I glass dry white wine
I small onion, sliced	Salt and pepper
50g/2 oz butter	Small handful of parsley
2 tablespoons olive oil	I clove of garlic
Flour	Strip of lemon peel
4 veal shins (about 800g/I ½ lb)	

In a pan large enough to hold the ossobuco in one layer, soften the onion in half the butter and the oil. Flour the veal shins lightly, roll up and tie with colourless thread. Moisten with white wine and add to the pan. When the wine has evaporated, season, and continue to cook gently, adding a little water or stock, if necessary, and not letting the meat stick to the pan. □ □ Trim and chop the parsley and garlic and add to the ossobuco together with the lemon peel halfway through cooking time. Continue cooking gently until the meat is done. Heat a serving dish and arrange the ossobuco on it, discarding the lemon rind. Mix the remaining butter into the sauce and pour over the ossobuco. Serve with saffron risotto.

ARROSTO DI MANZO ALLA CANNELLA
Pot-roast beef with cinnamon

Ingredients/serves 4	Salt and pepper
3 onions, thickly sliced	A pinch of cinnamon
75g/3 oz butter	Juice of 1 lemon
2 tablespoons oil	1 glass dry white wine
800g/1 ¾ lb loin of beef	1 bay leaf

LAZIO, UMBRIA AND THE MARCHES

P ut the onions into a pan with the butter and oil. Cook on a low heat for 5 minutes. Add the meat, season and sprinkle with cinnamon. Pour on the lemon juice and wine, add the bay leaf and cover with a lid. Cook over a low heat for 2½ hours, turning the meat every so often. When it is tender, remove the meat from the pot, slice and arrange on a serving dish. Pour over the hot sauce from the pan, top with the onions and serve. *Photograph page 184*

CARBONATA ALLA PIEMONTESE
Beef in red wine

Ingredients/serves 4	Salt and pepper
75g/3 oz lard *or* butter	200ml/⅓ pt meat sauce *or*
800g/1 ¾ lb beef, cut into cubes	extract of beef diluted in stock
500g/1 lb onions, sliced	A robust red wine, to cover

PIEDMONT

P reheat the oven to 190°C/375°F/Gas 5. Heat the lard or butter in a saucepan and brown the meat in it. Remove with a slotted spoon and transfer to a plate. Then add the onions to the pan and soften without letting them brown. (Add a few spoons of water if necessary.) When they are very soft, transfer to a casserole and put the meat on top. Season with salt and pepper and add the meat sauce. Then just cover with wine. □ □ Cook in the oven until the sauce is well reduced and the meat is tender (about 1 hour) and serve with hot polenta.

ARROSTO DI MANZO ALLA CANNELLA

POT-ROAST BEEF WITH CINNAMON
For recipe, see p.183

BEEF ESCALOPES WITH CAPERS
For recipe, see p.186

Scaloppine di Bue con Capperi

Beef escalopes with capers

LOMBARDY

Ingredients/serves 4	Oil
8 thinly sliced beef tenderloins	50g/2oz capers
(about 100g/4oz each)	1 tablespoon chopped parsley
Salt and pepper	2-3 tablespoons vinegar
Flour	Nutmeg
75g/3oz butter	

Beat the beef slices lightly into a regular shape, season and flour. Heat the butter with a little oil in a pan. Brown the escalopes, add the capers and parsley and 2 tablespoons cold water and cook, stirring frequently. In a separate pan heat the vinegar with the nutmeg on a brisk heat, pour over the meat and stir again. Serve the escalopes well covered in sauce. *Photograph page 185*

Bistecche di Manzo alle Acciughe

Steak with anchovies

LAZIO, UMBRIA AND THE MARCHES

Ingredients/serves 4	Salt and pepper
8 anchovy fillets	4 steaks weighing 100g/4oz
100g/4oz butter	each
	100g/4oz pitted green olives

Puree half the anchovies in a blender or press through a sieve and put in a bowl. Roll the others up and reserve. Add half the butter and a pinch of pepper to the anchovies and mix with a wooden spoon to a smooth paste. Shape the mixture into a sausage and wrap in aluminium foil. Refrigerate for 1 hour. ☐ ☐ Melt 1 tablespoon butter in a pan and add the steaks. Cook on a high flame for 2 minutes on each side. Drain, put on a dish, season and keep warm. Add the remaining butter to the cooking juices, stir in the olives and cook gently for 10 minutes, stirring occasionally. ☐ ☐ Take the anchovy butter from the refrigerator and cut into slices. Put a slice on each steak and top with a rolled anchovy. Garnish with olives, pour over the hot sauce and serve. *Photograph page 189*

BISTECCHE DI MANZO CON PROSCIUTTO E UOVA

Steak with ham and eggs

Ingredients/serves 4	Salt and pepper
75g/3oz butter	4 slices prosciutto
4 steaks	4 eggs

EMILIA-ROMAGNA

Melt half the butter in a pan and add the steaks. Cook briskly for 2 minutes each side. Drain, season and keep hot. Put the remaining butter into the pan. When it has melted, add the prosciutto and cook gently for 2 minutes. Break an egg onto each slice of ham and cook until the whites have set. Season the eggs and lift out the prosciutto with a flat spatula. Top the steaks with prosciutto and eggs and pour over the juices from the pan. Serve at once.

BISTECCHE DI MANZO CON BURRO DI GORGONZOLA

Steaks with gorgonzola butter

Ingredients/serves 4	1 tablespoon chopped parsley
75g/3oz butter, softened	A little lemon juice
50g/2oz mild gorgonzola cheese	4 steaks weighing 100g/4oz each
	Salt and pepper

EMILIA-ROMAGNA

Put 50g/2oz butter, the gorgonzola, parsley and a few drops of lemon juice into a bowl and mix well with a wooden spoon until the mixture is smooth and creamy. Roll it into a sausage shape and wrap in aluminium foil. Refrigerate for 1 hour. □ □ Melt the remaining butter in a pan and put in the steaks. Cook on a high flame for 2 minutes on each side. Drain, season and put on a serving dish. Cut the gorgonzola butter into slices and put 3 slices on each steak. Serve at once.

Photograph page 189

STEAKS WITH GORGONZOLA BUTTER
For recipe, see p.187

STEAK WITH ANCHOVIES
For recipe, see p.186

POLPETTONCINI ALLA NAPOLETANA FRITTI

Croquettes with mozzarella and lemon

CAMPANIA

Ingredients/serves 4	Salt and pepper
500g/1 lb lean minced beef	2 eggs, beaten
5 large slices stale crustless bread, soaked and squeezed	200g/7oz mozzarella cheese, diced
50g/2oz parsley, chopped	Flour
6 tablespoons grated parmesan cheese	Oil
	Lemon wedges

Combine the meat, bread, parsley and parmesan in a bowl, season and bind with the egg. Form into 4 croquettes and press the mozzarella into them. Reform. Roll in flour and fry in plenty of hot oil. Serve with lemon wedges.

Photograph page 200

POLPETTONICINI ALLA NAPOLETANA CON POMODORO

Croquettes with mozzarella and tomato

CAMPANIA

Ingredients/serves 4	2 eggs, beaten
500g/1lb lean minced beef	500g/1 lb mozzarella cheese, diced
5 large slices stale crustless bread, soaked in water and squeezed	Flour
	Oil
50g/2oz parsley, chopped	2 tablespoons chopped onion
6 tablespoons grated parmesan	500g/1lb tomatoes, skinned, deseeded, chopped and sieved
Salt and pepper	Basil

In a bowl mix the meat, bread, parsley and parmesan. Season and bind with the eggs. ☐ ☐ Divide the mixture into 4 and shape into oblongs on a damp marble slab. Press the mozzarella into the croquettes and reshape. Coat in flour and fry in plenty of hot oil. ☐ ☐ Meanwhile fry the onion in a pan with a few tablespoons of oil, add the tomato, season and cook on a moderate heat for about 20 minutes. Arrange the croquettes in the simmering sauce and leave to absorb the flavours, scooping the sauce on top. Garnish with coarsely chopped basil.

Photograph page 200

Spiedini di Carne con Funghi e Prugne

Beef kebabs with mushrooms and prunes

Ingredients/serves 4	
16 prunes	8 bay leaves
12 cubes lean beef about 40g/1½ oz each	Salt and pepper
	1 teaspoon powdered thyme
12 mushroom tops	Olive oil

LAZIO, UMBRIA
AND
THE MARCHES

Soak the prunes in tepid water for 1 hour, then drain and stone. Pre-heat the oven to 220°C/425°F/Gas 7. ☐ ☐ Thread the prunes, beef cubes and mushrooms alternately onto 4 metal skewers. Put a bay leaf at either end of each skewer. Season with salt, pepper and thyme and sprinkle the kebabs with olive oil. Put in an oiled baking dish and cook in the oven for 10 minutes, turning and basting with the cooking juices. Transfer to a serving dish and serve very hot.

Agnello Arrosto con Salsa di Fave

Roast lamb with broad bean sauce

Ingredients/serves 4	
255g/8oz podded broad beans	A sprig of rosemary
2 cloves of garlic	4 sage leaves
75g/3oz grated parmesan cheese	1kg/2 lb leg of lamb
	Salt and pepper
1 glass olive oil	

TUSCANY

Preheat the oven to 190°C/375°F/Gas 5. Pound the beans to a smooth paste with 1 clove garlic, the cheese and half the oil. Put the other clove of garlic, the rosemary, sage and remaining oil into an ovenproof casserole. Cook gently on top of the stove for 5 minutes, add the lamb and brown on all sides. Season and cook in the oven for 1½ hours, turning and basting the meat occasionally. ☐ ☐ When cooked, transfer to a serving dish and keep warm. Stir the bean purée into the juices in the casserole, and heat through. Pour into a sauce boat and serve with the lamb.

Photograph page 193

ROAST LAMB WITH LIMA BEAN SAUCE
For recipe, see p.191

RAGU DI AGNELLO AI CARCIOFI

LAMB AND ARTICHOKE CASSEROLE
For recipe, see p.194

COSTOLETTINE DI AGNELLO CON FUNGHI

Lamb cutlets in mushroom sauce

*LAZIO, UMBRIA
AND
THE MARCHES*

Ingredients/serves 4	
8 lamb cutlets	100g/4oz fresh mushrooms, sliced
75g/3oz butter	Salt and pepper
Salt	Nutmeg
2 eggs, beaten	Dry white wine
Breadcrumbs	200ml/⅓pt concentrated veal *or* chicken stock
A handful of chopped parsley	1 tablespoon flour
150ml/¼pt homemade tomato sauce	2 egg yolks
For the sauce	1 carton single cream
½ small onion, chopped	Squeeze of lemon juice
75g/3oz butter	

Fry the onion in half the butter, add the mushrooms, season with salt, pepper and nutmeg, moisten with a little white wine and cook, adding half the stock gradually. ☐ ☐ Melt the remaining butter in a pan, mix in the flour and gradually blend into the remaining hot stock, reserving a few spoonfuls. Add the mushrooms cooking liquor to the sauce, the egg yolks, the reserved stock, cream and lemon juice. Adjust the seasoning and cook over a low flame until the sauce has thickened. (Do not allow it to boil.) ☐ ☐ Cook the cutlets, browning them in half the butter. Season, remove from the pan and allow to cool. Dip the cutlets in the beaten egg, then in the breadcrumbs. Heat the remaining butter in the pan and brown the breaded cutlets. Drain and serve with fried parsley.

RAGU DI AGNELLO AI CARCIOFI

Lamb and artichoke casserole

*LAZIO, UMBRIA
AND
THE MARCHES*

Ingredients/serves 4	
750g/1½ lb lamb, boned and cubed	Salt and pepper
	Stock
100g/4oz butter	8 artichoke hearts
Oil	1 glass dry white wine
	Parsley

Brown the meat in half the butter and a little oil, season and simmer gently until cooked, adding a little stock, if necessary. Blanch the artichoke hearts, cut into strips and cook in the remaining butter with a pinch of salt. ☐ ☐ Put the lamb onto a dish, add the wine to the cooking juices and reduce. Pour the sauce over the lamb, garnish with artichokes, sprinkle with parsley and serve. *Photograph page 193*

AGNELLO IN AGRODOLCE ALLA SICILIANA

Sweet and sour lamb

Ingredients/serves 4	Salt and pepper
2 lb lamb in one piece	1 lb tomatoes, peeled, crushed
2 cloves of garlic	and strained
A sprig of rosemary	½ glass wine vinegar
½ onion, sliced	4 teaspoons sugar
Oil	

SICILY

Wash lamb, dry and stick with slivers of garlic and leaves of rosemary. Fry onion in a flameproof casserole with a few spoonfuls of oil, brown meat, season and add strained tomato flesh. Cover and cook for 1½ hours. □ □ Halfway through cooking time, add vinegar and let some evaporate. Then add sugar and complete cooking time, adding a few spoonfuls of water or stock, if necessary. Serve meat sliced and well covered with hot sauce.

SPIEDINI RUSTICI E RISO IN FORNO

Baked country kebabs with rice

Ingredients/serves 4	Salt and pepper
500g/1 lb leg of pork	Flour
3 courgettes	Oil
100g/4oz mushrooms	1 onion, chopped
2 firm tomatoes	1 glass dry white wine
3 peppers	300g/10oz rice

LAZIO, UMBRIA
AND
THE MARCHES

Cut the meat, courgettes, mushrooms, tomatoes and peppers into slices. Thread them alternately onto 4 wooden kebab sticks. Season and flour lightly. Heat some oil in a pan and fry the kebabs. Add the onion and pour in half the wine. Cover and cook for 10 minutes, without reducing the sauce. Preheat the oven to 200°C/400°F/Gas 6. □ □ Add the rice, cover with the remaining wine and a little water, if necessary. Adjust the seasoning and bring to the boil, stirring. Cover, then put in the oven for 20 minutes. Let it stand for 5 minutes, then serve.

Photograph page 196

BAKED COUNTRY KEBABS WITH RICE
For recipe, see p.195

PROSCIUTTO FRESCO DI MAIALE SALSATO

HAM SLICES WITH ANCHOVY SAUCE
For recipe, see p.199

COSCIOTTO DI MAIALE AL FORNO
Roast leg of pork

LAZIO, UMBRIA AND THE MARCHES

Ingredients/serves 4	
1 leg of pork with fat, about 1.5kg/3lb	200ml/^{2}/₃pt stock
1 glass olive oil	75g/3oz sugar
200g/7oz pork rind	600ml/1pt dry white wine
Salt and pepper	1 tablespoon cloves
	4 tablespoons vinegar
	1 teaspoon cornflour

S oak the pork leg in cold water for 2 hours, then drain. Preheat the oven to 160°C/325°F/Gas 3. Pour the oil into a large casserole and put in the pork rind. Season the meat and add to the casserole. Cook in the oven for 6 hours, basting occasionally with a little boiling stock. ☐ ☐ Drain the leg over a plate, remove the rind from the pan and skim the fat from the gravy. With a sharp knife, cut crosses into the rind of the meat, put a clove into each cross and sprinkle with sugar. Put the leg back into the roasting pan and return to the oven at 190°C/375°F/Gas 5 until the sugar caramelizes. ☐ ☐ Mix the wine with the vinegar and the cooking juices from the pan and pour this mixture over the meat. Cook for a further hour. ☐ ☐ Transfer the pork to a serving dish. Skim the cooking juices, strain and bring to boiling point. Add the cornflour and thicken the gravy. Pour it into a sauce boat and serve with the meat.

COSTOLETTE DI MAIALE ALLE OLIVE
Pork chops with olives

LAZIO, UMBRIA AND THE MARCHES

Ingredients/serves 4	
200g/7 oz large pitted olives	Salt and pepper
20 cloves of garlic	75g/3 oz lard
4 pork chops	4 tablespoons Marsala *or* white wine
Oil	4 tablespoons meat sauce *or* 2 teaspoons meat extract
Vinegar	1 tablespoon chopped parsley
A sprig of rosemary	
A few leaves of sage	

B oil the olives in water for 10 minutes, remove from the heat and keep hot in their cooking liquor. Peel 18 cloves of garlic, cook for 3 minutes in boiling water, then drain. Flatten the chops and insert the remaining garlic, cut into slivers. Prepare a marinade with the oil, a little vinegar, the rosemary and sage, salt and pepper. Put the chops in the marinade and leave for a couple of hours, turning occasionally, then drain and pat dry. ☐ ☐ Heat the lard in a pan with 1 tablespoon oil and put in the chops. Let them brown for 3 minutes on each side. Lower the heat, add the garlic and carry on cooking for 12 minutes, stirring occassionally. Put the chops on a plate and pile the garlic and olives in the centre. ☐ ☐ Pour the Marsala into the cooking juices, let it reduce a little, add the meat sauce (or the extract diluted in a little hot water) and simmer for 5 minutes, then pour the sauce onto the chops. Sprinkle with chopped parsley and serve. *Photograph page 200*

PROSCIUTTO FRESCO DI MAIALE SALSATO

Ham slices with anchovy sauce

EMILIA-
ROMAGNA

Ingredients/serves 4	1 small onion, chopped
8 slices ham, 75g/3 oz each	5 anchovy fillets de-salted and pounded
Salt and pepper	
Flour	1 tablespoon pickled capers, chopped
2 eggs, beaten	
A few tablespoons soft breadcrumbs	1 tablespoon chopped parsley
	A little vinegar
100g/4 oz butter	A little stock

F latten the ham slices with a mallet, season, then dip in flour, egg and breadcrumbs. Put half the butter on to heat, add the onion and cook gently until soft. Add the anchovy fillets, capers, parsley, 1 tablespoon flour and a little pepper. Stir over a high heat for a few minutes, thin with 2-3 tablespoons vinegar and let evaporate. Add enough stock to give a slightly thickened sauce. Continue to stir the sauce and add 25g/1 oz butter, diced, making sure that each piece is fully incorporated before adding the next. ☐ ☐ In a separate pan heat the remaining butter, put in the breaded ham slices, brown on both sides, lower the heat and cook for 10-12 minutes, turning once. ☐ ☐ Lay the ham on a serving dish, pour over the hot sauce and serve accompanied with buttered spinach. *Photograph page 197*

POLPETTONCINI ALLA NAPOLETANA CON POMODORO
POLPETTONCINI ALLA NAPOLETANA FRITTI

CROQUETTES WITH MOZZARELLA AND TOMATO (TOP)
AND WITH MOZZARELLA AND LEMON (BOTTOM)
For recipes, see p.190

COSTOLETTE DI MAIALE ALLE OLIVE

PORK CHOPS WITH OLIVES
For recipe, see p.198

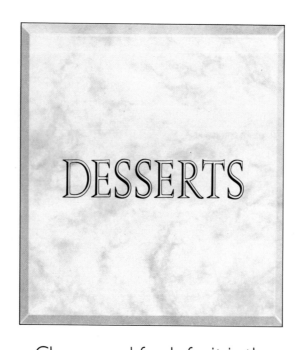

DESSERTS

Cheese and fresh fruit is the traditional Italian dessert for everyday, but on Sundays and special occasions lunch can be rounded off with elaborate concoctions of cream, chocolate and meringue on a sponge base soaked in liqueur. In addition to some of the sumptuous Italian desserts that can be made at home, this section also includes a selection of dessert cookies. These can be eaten in Italy at any time of the day — nibbled with coffee or an early morning glass of wine, or enjoyed after a heavy meal with a warming and syrupy liqueur.

FRAGOLINI FRITTI
Fried strawberries

Ingredients/serves 6	
75g/3oz flour	550g/1 lb strawberries
40g/1½oz butter, melted	75g/3oz sugar
1 egg and 1 egg white	1 small glass maraschino
Milk	Oil for deep-frying
1 small glass brandy	50g/2oz icing sugar

LAZIO, UMBRIA AND THE MARCHES

Sift the flour into a bowl and mix in the butter. Add the egg, milk and brandy and mix to a smooth batter. Leave to stand for an hour. Trim, wash and spread out the strawberries on a plate. Sprinkle with the sugar and maraschino and leave to macerate. ☐ ☐ Ten minutes before serving beat the egg white until stiff and fold into the batter. Dip the strawberries into the batter one by one, coating well, and deep-fry in plenty of oil. When golden brown and crisp, drain on paper towels. Put on a dish, sprinkle with icing sugar and serve. *Photograph page 205*

RAVIOLI DOLCI AL FORNO
Sweet baked ravioli

Ingredients/serves 6-8	For the filling
For the pasta	400g/14oz chestnuts
600g/1¼lb flour	100g/4oz bitter cocoa
100g/4oz butter	50g/2oz sugar
100g/4oz sugar	100g/4oz chopped almonds
4 eggs	100g/4oz amaretti biscuits,
1 tablespoon fresh yeast	crumbled
150ml/¼pt milk	200g/7oz orange marmalade

CAMPANIA

For the pasta, mix together the flour, butter, sugar, 3 eggs and the yeast dissolved in tepid milk. Knead the dough for 20 minutes and wrap in a tea towel. Leave to rise for an hour. ☐ ☐ For the filling, boil the chestnuts, peel, press through a sieve or blend in a liquidizer, and mix with the cocoa, sugar, almonds, amaretti and marmalade. Combine well. ☐ ☐ Roll out the pasta into a thin sheet and cut into circles 5cm/2 inches in diameter. Place some filling on each and close into a semicircle. Arrange on a greased baking sheet and brush with beaten egg. Bake at 180°C/350°F/Gas 4 for 20 minutes. *Photograph page 205*

FRIED STRAWBERRIES
For recipe, see p.203

SWEET BAKED RAVIOLI
For recipe, see p.203

RISO DOLCE DI SAN GIUSEPPE ALLA TOSCANA

Sweet rice croquettes San Giuseppe

TUSCANY

Ingredients/serves 4	50g/2oz seedless raisins,
100g/4oz flour	soaked and chopped
15g/½ oz fresh yeast	25g/1oz pine nuts
600ml/1pt milk	25g/1oz caster sugar
100g/4oz rice	Grated rind of ½ lemon
2 egg yolks and 1 egg	Oil for frying
Pinch of salt	Icing sugar

Mix half the flour with the crumbled yeast and enough tepid milk to form a dough. Knead into a ball and mark a cross on top. Put the dough in a bowl and moisten the top with milk. Let it rise in a warm place for 20-30 minutes, until doubled in size. □ □ Pour the remaining milk into a pan, bring to the boil, add the rice and cook, uncovered, over a moderate heat. When cooked, pour into a bowl and allow to cool, then add the remaining flour, egg yolks and egg, salt, dough, raisins, pine nuts, caster sugar and lemon rind and stir well, adding a few tablespoons of milk, if necessary. □ □ Heat some oil in a pan, shape the rice mixture into balls and fry, without letting them touch. When golden brown, drain on paper towels, dust with icing sugar and serve. *Photograph page 208*

SFOGLIATELLE NAPOLETANE
Ricotta roll

CAMPANIA

Ingredients/serves 2-4	For the filling
For the pastry	1 egg and 3 yolks
250g/8oz flour	100g/4oz caster sugar
50g/2oz butter or margarine	1 tablespoon cornflour
2 tablespoons sugar	300ml/½pt hot milk
2 eggs	A few drops of vanilla
Pinch of salt	flavouring
Milk	150g/5oz fresh ricotta
Icing sugar	25g/1oz candied orange peel

Combine the ingredients for the pastry, adding enough milk to give a soft elastic consistency. Knead well and chill for 30 minutes. For the filling, beat the yolks with the caster sugar, add the cornflour and gradually mix in the milk and vanilla flavouring. Put in a pan over a gentle heat until it comes to the boil, stirring constantly. Remove from the heat, allow to cool, add the ricotta, orange peel and egg, diluted with a few drops of water or liqueur. □ □ Roll out the pastry onto a floured board, then cut into rectangles. Put the filling on half the rectangles and cover with the other half, sealing the edges firmly. Brush with beaten egg, if desired. Arrange on a greased, floured baking sheet and bake at 190°C/375°F/Gas 5. When golden brown, remove from the oven and dust with icing sugar. *Photograph page 208*

POMPELMI E ARANCE IN INSALATA
Orange and grapefruit salad

CAMPANIA

Ingredients/serves 4	
2 large oranges	Caster sugar
3 large ripe grapefruit	Sweet liqueur

Peel the oranges and grapefruit and remove the pith. Cut into slices, then cut in half and arrange in a crystal bowl. Pour on the juice left on the cutting board and add plenty of sugar and your choice of liqueur. Chill for at least an hour before serving. *Photograph page 209*

*S*WEET RICE CROQUETTES SAN GIUSEPPE
For recipe, see p.206

SFOGLIATELLE NAPOLETANE

*R*ICOTTA ROLL
For recipe, see p.207

POMPELMI E ARANCE IN INSALATA

*O*RANGE AND GRAPEFRUIT SALAD
For recipe, see p.207

TIMBALLO CON LE PERE ALLA PIEMONTESE

*T*IMBALE OF PEARS IN RED WINE
For recipe, see p.210

TIMBALLO CON LE PERE ALLA PIEMONTESE

Timbale of pears in red wine

PIEDMONT

Ingredients/serves 4	For the filling
For the pastry	500g/1 lb pears
200g/7 oz flour	Red wine
100g/4 oz sugar	Sugar
100g/4 oz corn meal	1 clove
150g/5 oz butter	A pinch of cinnamon
A pinch of salt	
3 egg yolks	

Cut the pears into pieces and cook them in red wine with a little sugar and the spices. To make the pastry, combine the flour, sugar, cornmeal, butter (except for one small knob), salt and egg yolks, adding a little water, if necessary. Chill, then roll out and line a baking tin. Fill with the pears. Cover the timbale with a pastry lattice and bake at 190°C/375°F/Gas 5, until golden brown. *Photograph page 209*

ZABAIONE

Zabaglione

EMILIA-ROMAGNA

Ingredients/per person	1 heaped tablespoon sugar
1 egg, separated	2 tablespoons dry Marsala

You can substitute dry white wine, Malaga or port for the Marsala. If you use a liqueur, it is best to halve the quantity and add half dry white wine. Zabaione can be served with whipped cream or wafer biscuits, or it can be used to accompany other desserts. Put the egg yolk into a small pan (copper, if possible) over a medium flame. Add the sugar and beat well with a whisk or wooden spoon. Gradually add the Marsala, stirring continuously, then either lower the heat or transfer the pan to a bain marie (the easier method), and keep stirring until the mixture has risen and is light and fluffy. Make sure the heat is not too high — if it is, you will feel the mixture catching on the bottom. If it does, remove the pan from the heat for a short time. □ □ To serve, pour into a dish and allow to cool — never leave it in the pan. If it is to be served cold, you should put a circle of waxed paper over it, touching the surface.

RICOTTA FRITTA ALLA ROMANA
Ricotta fritters

LAZIO, UMBRIA AND THE MARCHES

Ingredients/serves 4	
500g/1 lb ricotta cheese	Oil
A little flour	100g/4 oz sugar
2 eggs, beaten	A pinch of ground cinnamon

C ut the ricotta into cubes about the thickness of a finger and 5cm/2 inches square, roll them in flour and then in beaten egg. Fry in a wide pan with plenty of hot oil. When golden brown, drain, arrange on a serving dish and sprinkle with sugar mixed with cinnamon.

PANFORTE DI SIENA
Sienese spicecake

TUSCANY

Ingredients/serves 10-12	
1 tablespoon coriander seeds	500g/1 lb shelled almonds
50g/2 oz unsweetened cocoa powder	50g/2 oz shelled walnuts
2 tablespoons cinnamon	150g/5 oz candied orange peel
1 nutmeg	50g/2 oz candied citrus peel
3 cinnamon sticks	500g/1 lb candied melon peel
1/2 teaspoon cloves	100g/4 oz honey
6 black peppercorns	250g/8 oz caster sugar
	150g/5 oz flour

F irst prepare two powders: pound the coriander in a mortar and mix half this with the cocoa and ground cinnamon. □ □ Grate the nutmeg, and grind it together with the cinnamon sticks, cloves, pepper and remaining coriander. Set aside. □ □ Toast the almonds at 180°C/350°F/Gas 4 in a pre-heated oven. Keep the oven on at this temperature. Chop the walnuts finely. Coarsely chop the candied fruit. □ □ Put the honey and caster sugar in a copper pan over heat, stirring continuously until the sugar has reached the 'ball' stage. Remove from the heat, stir in the candied fruit, then the almonds, walnuts, sifted flour and spice mixtures. □ □ Divide the mixture and spread into circles about 2.5cm/1 inch high. Use a pie dish to cut the circles out. Fasten a double thickness of paper round the edge of each circle to keep it in shape on a baking sheet. Bake for 30 minutes. □ □ Allow to cool before removing from the tray. Remove the paper with scissors. Dust with the icing sugar mixed with cinnamon, if liked.

SICILIAN *TRIFLE CAKE*
For recipe, see p.215

SLAVIC *FRUIT CAKE*
For recipe, see p.216

*G*ENOESE-STYLE SPONGE CAKE
For recipe, see p.218

BRUTTI MA BUONI!

*U*GLY BUT NICE!
For recipe, see p.219

ZUCCOTTO
Cream sponge deluxe

TUSCANY

Ingredients/serves 8-10	Rind of 1 lemon, grated
6 eggs	75g/3 oz flour
175g/6 oz caster sugar	75g/3 oz potato starch
For the filling	900ml/1 ½ pt fresh cream
250g/8 oz chocolate	A few drops vanilla flavouring
25g/1 oz hazelnuts	150g/5 oz icing sugar
25g/1 oz sweet almonds	Sweet cocoa powder
Small glass liqueur plus 2 tbsp	Glacé cherries (optional)

Y ou can buy the chocolate decorations instead of making them. Prepare the cake the day before eating, as it will slice better. Grease and flour a deep cake tin, 10 inches in diameter. Preheat the oven to 190°C/375°F/Gas 5. ☐ ☐ Beat the eggs and sugar together until very frothy with an electric mixer, if possible. Then add the lemon rind and sift in the flour. Fold in the potato starch. Turn into the cake tin and bake for 40 minutes. Cool on a rack. ☐ ☐ Melt the chocolate over a low heat and pour into a greaseproof paper cornet with a fine, open end. Pipe tiny circles of chocolate onto a sheet of greaseproof paper and let them cool and set. Pour the rest of the chocolate onto another sheet in a thin layer and allow to cool. When it no longer marks when touched, cut out circles with a pastry cutter. Then upturn the sheet onto another so that the circles fall onto it and reserve the chocolate trimmings for use later. ☐ ☐ Toast the hazelnuts in the oven and brush off the skins. Blanch and peel the almonds and chop the nuts together finely. ☐ ☐ Cut 2 greaseproof paper strips and put into a 2lt/3½ pt mould to help lift out the dessert. Pour a little liqueur into a bowl. Cut the cake in half horizontally, cut off a layer, then line the mould with the rest of the cake and soak it with liqueur. ☐ ☐ Melt the chocolate trimmings. Pour 600ml/1 pt cream into a bowl and whip. Then mix in the tiny chocolate drops, almonds, hazelnuts, vanilla flavouring, half the icing sugar and 2 tablespoons liqueur. Mix well, then pour half the mixture into the mould and level off. Add the melted chocolate to the other half, and pour this too into the mould. Cover with a greaseproof paper circle and push down the mixture with a piece of cardboard. Chill for 4 hours or more. ☐ ☐ Upturn the pudding onto a sheet of greaseproof paper and remove all the paper. Dredge with the remaining icing sugar. Then place 4 paper strips, each 2.5cm/1 inch wide, over the top of the cake, crossing them and tucking the edges underneath it. Sift the cocoa over the spaces and carefully remove the paper. ☐ ☐ Put two spatulas underneath the cake and lift it onto a serving dish. Whip the remaining cream and pipe tufts of cream around and on top of the zuccotto. Decorate with chocolate discs and glacé cherries, if desired, and chill until time to serve.

CASSATA ALLA SICILIANA
Sicilian trifle cake

SICILY

Ingredients/serves 8-10	For the topping
750g/1 ½ lb ricotta	3 tablespoons apricot jelly
15g/½ oz pistachio nuts	1 tablespoon icing sugar
150g/5 oz chocolate	300g/10 oz caster sugar
200g/7 oz mixed candied peel	1 tablespoon glucose
1 loaf gingerbread	Orange flower water
500g/1 lb caster sugar	200g/7 oz mixed candied peel
A few drops vanilla flavouring	
A pinch of cinnamon	

L ine with greaseproof paper a hinged cake tin about 25cm/10 inches in diameter. Press the ricotta through a sieve into a bowl. Blanch and peel the pistachios and pound in a mortar. Chop the chocolate and candied peel. Cut the gingerbread into slices and line the cake tin with it, reserving a few slices. ☐ ☐ Put half the caster sugar and a few tablespoons water on to heat until the sugar has dissolved. ☐ ☐ Beat the ricotta, adding the dissolved cooled sugar, vanilla, cinnamon, chocolate, candied peel and nuts. Put the mixture into the cake tin, cover with the remaining gingerbread slices and then another layer of greaseproof paper. Push down and chill for a few hours. ☐ ☐ Meanwhile make the topping. Melt the apricot jelly, add the sugar and heat until threads form when a spoon is raised from the mixture. Remove the cake tin from the refrigerator and upturn onto a dish. Cover the cassata with the jelly mixture. ☐ ☐ On a low heat melt the remaining caster sugar and the glucose, adding a few tablespoons of orange flower water. Stir well, then pour onto the middle of the cake and spread all over it with a spatula. Decorate the cake with the candied peel and let the topping set. Using 2 spatulas lift the cake onto a serving dish. *Photograph page 212*

POTIZZA ALLA FRUTTA SECCA
Slavic fruit cake

VENETO

Ingredients/serves 4	125g/5oz walnut kernels
25g/1oz fresh yeast	100g/4oz sultanas
Salt	150ml/¼ pt rum
100g/4oz sugar	100g/4oz butter
600ml/1pt milk	250g/8oz caster sugar
750g/1½ lb self-rising flour	4 eggs, separated
100g/4oz butter	Small carton of whipping
3 egg yolks	cream, whipped
Grated rind of 1 lemon	Grated rind of 1 lemon
For the filling	A Pinch of cinnamon
100g/4oz peeled hazelnuts	Beaten egg

For the pastry, crumble the yeast into a cup, add a pinch of salt, the sugar and tepid milk (reserving a few tablespoons). Put the flour in a bowl, add the yeast mixture and half the butter and mix well together. Make the dough into a ball and put in a floured bowl. Cut a cross on the surface, cover the dough with a tea towel and leave to rise in a warm place. When risen to twice its original size, add the yolks mixed with the remaining milk, remaining butter cut into pieces and the grated lemon rind. Knead the dough and let it rise to double in volume again. Then knead and repeat once more. ☐ ☐ For the filling, bake the hazelnuts and skin them, then chop with the walnuts. Soak the sultanas in the rum. Cream the butter with half the sugar. Beat the yolks with the rest of the sugar until frothy. Add to the butter and sugar, fold in the whipped cream, lemon rind and cinnamon. Add the drained sultanas and half the chopped nuts. Beat the egg whites until stiff and fold in. ☐ ☐ Roll out the cake mix on a floured board. Cut into 3 oblongs, the length of the baking sheet. Spread the filling onto these, adding the remaining nuts. Roll lengthwise, brush with beaten egg and place on a greased baking sheet. Allow to rise for a further 15 minutes, then bake at 190°C/375°F/Gas 5 for an hour. *Photograph page 212*

STRUFFOLI ALLA PARTENOPEA
Honeyed Neapolitan doughnuts

Ingredients/serves 4	1 tablespoon brandy
350g/12oz flour	Salt
3 eggs	A little milk
100g/4oz sugar	Oil
25g/1oz butter	150g/5oz honey
A little grated orange and lemon peel	40g/1½oz hundreds and thousands
100g/4oz candied citrus peel, diced	

CAMPANIA

Mix the flour with the beaten eggs, 25g/1oz sugar, the butter, orange and lemon peel, half the candied citrus peel, the brandy and a pinch of salt (adding a little milk, if necessary). Shape the dough into a ball, cover with a tea towel and leave to stand for an hour. ☐ ☐ Make thin sticks of dough and deep fry in oil. Drain on paper towels when golden brown. ☐ ☐ Into a pan (copper, if possible) put the honey, remaining sugar, and a few spoons of water. Bring gently to the boil and cook until golden. Lower the heat and add the pastries, stirring continuously to coat in honey. Remove with a slotted spoon, put onto a wet dish, and mould with your hands into ring doughnut shapes. ☐ ☐ Sprinkle hundreds and thousands over them and decorate with the remaining candied peel cut into strips.

GENOISE
Genoese-style sponge cake

LIGURIA

Ingredients/serves 4	A few drops vanilla flavouring
75g/3oz butter, diced	*or* the rind of 1 lemon, grated
4 eggs	150g/5oz flour, sifted
125g/5oz caster sugar	1 tablespoon rum *or* cognac

Grease a 22-25cm/8-10 inch round cake tin and dust with flour. Melt the butter in a small saucepan. Preheat the oven to 180°C/350°F/Gas 4. □ □ Break the eggs into a copper saucepan, add the sugar and whisk for a moment. Put the pan on a low heat or in a bain marie. Remove from the heat and continue whisking, or use an electric beater. When the mixture has cooled, add vanilla or grated lemon rind, rum or cognac, and the flour. Mix well, then add the melted butter gradually, stirring, to prevent it sticking. Put the mixture in the cake tin — it should come a little more than half way up the sides — and bake for about 30 minutes. It is ready when the centre springs back when touched. Turn out onto a rack to cool. □ □ If you want to fill it, prepare the génoise a few days ahead of time, and store wrapped in greasproof paper. *Photograph page 213*

STRACA-DENT ALLA ROMAGNOLA
Munchies

EMILIA-ROMAGNA

Ingredients/makes 8	200g/7oz caster sugar
350g/12oz sweet almonds	3 egg whites
200g/7oz flour, sifted	

Preheat the oven to 180°C/350°F/Gas 4. □ □ Blanch and peel the almonds, toast lightly in the oven, then chop. Mix together the flour, almonds, sugar and beaten egg whites and knead with your hands until you have a smooth mixture. Grease a baking sheet and heap the mixture on it in small mounds. Bake until golden brown. Allow to cool completely, arrange on a pretty plate, then serve.

AMARETTI
Almond cookies

Makes 30 cookies	300g/10oz caster sugar
175g/6oz sweet almonds	A pinch of baking powder
100g/4oz bitter almonds	4 egg whites

CAMPANIA

Preheat the oven to 180°C/350°F/Gas 4. Put both kinds of almonds into a pan of cold water, bring to the boil, remove and skin, then put onto a baking sheet and into the oven to dry out, not letting them brown. Remove and let cool. Turn oven down to 140°C/275°F/Gas 1. □ □ Butter a baking sheet and flour it. Put the almonds and a little sugar in a mortar and pound to a powder. Pour the powder into a bowl with the rest of the sugar and the baking powder and stir. Beat the egg whites stiffly, then fold in the almonds. Pipe the mixture onto the baking sheet, making small heaps. Bake until well dried out (about 40 minutes) and allow to cool before serving.

BRUTTI MA BUONI
Ugly but nice!

Makes 50 cookies	200g/7oz icing sugar
225g/8oz sweet almonds	Ground cinnamon
3 egg whites	5 cloves, crushed to a powder
A few drops vanilla flavouring	

VENETO

Preheat the oven to 180°C/350°F/Gas 4. Blanch the almonds, skin, and then dry on a baking sheet in the oven, turning without letting them brown. Remove from the oven and reduce the temperature to 150°C/300°F/Gas 2. Chop the almonds finely. □ □ Beat the egg whites in a bowl until stiff, then fold in the chopped almonds, vanilla sugar, cinnamon and powdered cloves. Put walnut-sized pieces of the mixture onto a greased and floured baking sheet, not letting them touch. Bake for 40 minutes. Put on a rack or cloth to cool and store in an airtight container. *Photograph page 213*

INDEX

INDEX

Acknowledgements

The publishers gratefully acknowledge the kind assistance of the following: Gruppo Editoriale Fabbri, Milan, and, in particular, Virginia Prina for her helpfulness throughout the production of this book; Linda Sonntag for writing all introductory text and for her help at every editorial stage; Anna Nyburg for her translating skills; John Heseltine for additional photography; and Barbara Croxford.

Guide to uncaptioned photographs

Pp. 66-7, Florence; *p. 70*, Venice; *pp. 74-5*, Venice; *pp. 78-9*, Apucali, Lombardy; *pp. 84-5*, Florence; *pp. 88-9*, looking north-east from Castello di Cacchiano; *pp. 92-3*, Umbria; *pp. 100-1*, Ancona, the Marches; *pp. 104-5*, Florence; *pp. 108-9*, San Miniato, near Pisa; *pp. 114-5*, Celle di Macra, near Cuneo, Piedmont; *pp. 118-9*, Lombardy; *pp. 122-3*, San Gimignano, Tuscany; *pp. 126-7*, Rome; *pp. 134-5*, Amalfi; *pp. 138-9*, Castel Gardena; *pp. 142-3*, Padua; *pp. 148-9*, Emilia-Romagna; *pp. 152-3*, the Appenines, between Riolo and Brisighellia; *pp. 156-7*, Rieti, Umbria; *pp. 160-1*, Valcamonica, near Lake Garda, Lombardy; *pp. 164-5*, Bologna, Emilia-Romagna; *pp. 168-9*, Rome; *pp. 172-3*, Bari; *pp. 176-7*, Sorrento; *pp. 180-1*, Sicily; *pp. 184-5*, Bolzano; *pp. 188-9*, Grado, Friuli; *pp. 192-3*, Siena; *pp. 196-7*, the Tuscan countryside around San Gimignano; *pp. 200-1*, Cilento; *pp. 204-5*, Molise; *pp. 208-9*, Valle d'Aosta, Piedmont.

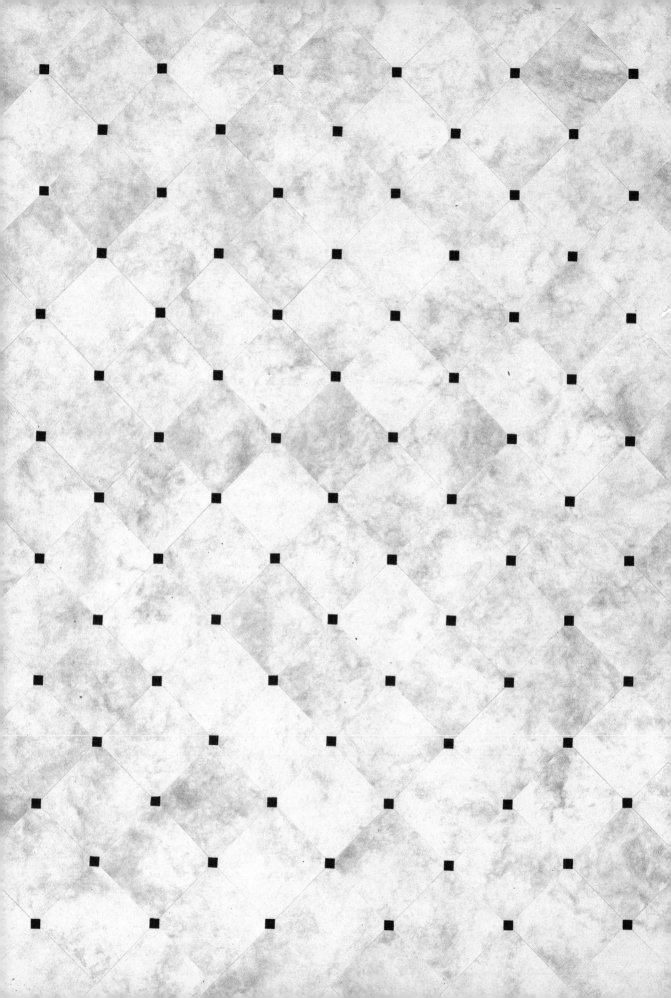